Defending an Open, Global, Secure, and Resilient Internet

COUNCIL *on* **FOREIGN RELATIONS**

Independent Task Force Report No. 70

John D. Negroponte and
Samuel J. Palmisano, *Chairs*
Adam Segal, *Project Director*

Defending an Open, Global, Secure, and Resilient Internet

The Council on Foreign Relations (CFR) is an independent, nonpartisan membership organization, think tank, and publisher dedicated to being a resource for its members, government officials, business executives, journalists, educators and students, civic and religious leaders, and other interested citizens in order to help them better understand the world and the foreign policy choices facing the United States and other countries. Founded in 1921, CFR carries out its mission by maintaining a diverse membership, with special programs to promote interest and develop expertise in the next generation of foreign policy leaders; convening meetings at its headquarters in New York and in Washington, DC, and other cities where senior government officials, members of Congress, global leaders, and prominent thinkers come together with CFR members to discuss and debate major international issues; supporting a Studies Program that fosters independent research, enabling CFR scholars to produce articles, reports, and books and hold roundtables that analyze foreign policy issues and make concrete policy recommendations; publishing *Foreign Affairs*, the preeminent journal on international affairs and U.S. foreign policy; sponsoring Independent Task Forces that produce reports with both findings and policy prescriptions on the most important foreign policy topics; and providing up-to-date information and analysis about world events and American foreign policy on its website, www.cfr.org.

The Council on Foreign Relations takes no institutional positions on policy issues and has no affiliation with the U.S. government. All views expressed in its publications and on its website are the sole responsibility of the author or authors.

The Council on Foreign Relations sponsors Independent Task Forces to assess issues of current and critical importance to U.S. foreign policy and provide policymakers with concrete judgments and recommendations. Diverse in backgrounds and perspectives, Task Force members aim to reach a meaningful consensus on policy through private and nonpartisan deliberations. Once launched, Task Forces are independent of CFR and solely responsible for the content of their reports. Task Force members are asked to join a consensus signifying that they endorse "the general policy thrust and judgments reached by the group, though not necessarily every finding and recommendation." Each Task Force member also has the option of putting forward an additional or dissenting view. Members' affiliations are listed for identification purposes only and do not imply institutional endorsement. Task Force observers participate in discussions, but are not asked to join the consensus.

For further information about CFR or this Task Force, please write to the Council on Foreign Relations, 58 East 68th Street, New York, NY 10065, or call the Communications office at 212.434.9888. Visit CFR's website at www.cfr.org.

This report is printed on paper that is FSC® certified by Rainforest Alliance, which promotes environmentally responsible, socially beneficial, and economically viable management of the world's forests.

MIX
Paper from
responsible sources
FSC® C015782

Task Force Members

Task Force members are asked to join a consensus signifying that they endorse "the general policy thrust and judgments reached by the group, though not necessarily every finding and recommendation." They participate in the Task Force in their individual, not institutional, capacities.

Elana Berkowitz
Etsy

Bob Boorstin
Google, Inc.

Jeff A. Brueggeman
AT&T

Peter Cleveland
Intel Corporation

Esther Dyson
EDventure Holdings, Inc.

Martha Finnemore
George Washington University

Patrick Gorman

Michael V. Hayden
Chertoff Group

Eugene J. Huang
American Express

Anthony P. Lee
Altos Ventures

Catherine B. Lotrionte
Georgetown University

Susan Markham Lyne
AOL, Inc.

Naotaka Matsukata
FairWinds Partners

Jeff Moss
Internet Corporation for Assigned Names and Numbers (ICANN)

Craig James Mundie
Microsoft Corporation

John D. Negroponte
McLarty Associates

Joseph S. Nye Jr.
Harvard University

Samuel J. Palmisano
IBM Corporation

Neal A. Pollard
PricewaterhouseCoopers LLP

Contents

Foreword

Over the course of the last four decades, the Internet has developed from an obscure government science experiment to one of the cornerstones of modern life. It has transformed commerce, created social and cultural networks with global reach, and become a surprisingly powerful vehicle for political organization and protest alike. And it has achieved all of this despite—or perhaps because of—its decentralized character. Throughout its public history, the Internet has been built and overseen by an international group of technical experts and government and user representatives committed to maintaining an open and unfettered global network.

This vision, however, and the Internet to which it gave rise, is under threat from a number of directions. States are erecting barriers to the free flow of information to and through their countries. Even Western governments do not always agree on common content standards—the United States, for example, is more accepting of neo-Nazi content or Holocaust denial than are France or Germany. Other countries' efforts to control the Internet have gone far beyond limiting hate speech or pornography. Iran, China, Saudi Arabia, Russia, and others have considered building national computer networks that would tightly control or even sever connections to the global Internet.

State and nonstate actors, moreover, now regularly attack the websites and internal systems of businesses. Most of these attacks are for theft—cost estimates of intellectual property losses range as high as $500 billion per year. Other activities are related to sabotage or espionage. Hacking and defacing websites or social media feeds is a frequently used tool of political competition, while destructive programs such as Stuxnet are becoming increasingly sophisticated. Such activities can be expected to become more commonplace as critical systems become more interconnected and financial and technical barriers to entry for cyber activities fall further.

A balkanized Internet beset by hostile cyber-related activities raises a host of questions and problems for the U.S. government, American corporations, and American citizens. The Council on Foreign Relations launched this Task Force to define the scope of this rapidly developing issue and to help shape the norms, rules, and laws that should govern the Internet.

The Task Force recommends that the United States develop a digital policy framework based on four pillars. First, it calls on the U.S. government to share leadership with like-minded actors, including governments, private companies, and NGOs, to develop a global security framework based on a common set of principles and practices. Next, the Task Force recommends that all future trade agreements between the United States and its trading partners contain a goal of fostering the free flow of information and data across national borders while protecting intellectual property and individual privacy. Third, the Task Force urges the U.S. government to define and actively promote a vision of Internet governance that involves emerging Internet powers and expands and strengthens governance processes that include representatives of governments, private industry, and civil society. Finally, the report recommends that U.S.-based industry work rapidly to establish an industry-led approach to counter current and future cyberattacks. The United States needs to act proactively on these fronts, lest it risk ceding the initiative to countries whose interests differ significantly from its own.

The Task Force further argues for greater public debate in the United States about cyber capabilities as instruments of national security. Some forty countries, including the United States, either have or are seeking cyber weapons. Greater public scrutiny and discussion will, among other things, help define the conditions under which cyber weapons might be used—conditions which should likely be highly limited in scope and subject to substantial oversight.

I would like to thank the Task Force's distinguished chairs, John Negroponte and Samuel Palmisano, for their leadership and commitment to this endeavor. This Task Force report is the product of an impressive group of individuals with significant experience and expertise in both the public and private sectors. I am grateful to all of the Task Force members and observers for contributing their time and informed perspectives to reach a consensus—one that reflects a broad range of political viewpoints and professional backgrounds.

I also invite readers to review the additional views written by several Task Force members that appear at the report's conclusion. The report of an Independent Task Force is a document that represents the consensus among the group, and each signatory endorses the broad thrust of the policy recommendations. However, these additional views provide insight into the breadth of the debate and demonstrate the complexity of the issues at hand.

My thanks also extend to Anya Schmemann, CFR's Task Force program director, whose guidance and direction made this project possible. I would finally like to thank Project Director and Maurice R. Greenberg Senior Fellow for China Studies Adam Segal, who expertly wove together the many perspectives represented by this Task Force in a report that is intended to educate people in the United States and beyond about the challenges we face in this digital age and how best to address them.

Richard N. Haass
President
Council on Foreign Relations
June 2013

Acknowledgments

The report of the Independent Task Force on U.S. Policy in the Digital Age is the product of the Task Force's members, who shared their time, expertise, and wisdom with us. I am sincerely grateful for their participation and guidance. In particular, I would like to thank our distinguished chairs, John D. Negroponte and Samuel J. Palmisano, for their strong leadership and thoughtful direction. It has been a pleasure to work with both of them.

Many Task Force members and observers offered detailed comments and feedback throughout the writing process, for which we are deeply appreciative. Special thanks go to Bob Boorstin, Peter Cleveland, Martha Finnemore, Tressa Steffen Guenov, Jeff Moss, Neal A. Pollard, Elliot J. Schrage, and Anne-Marie Slaughter, who went above and beyond the call of duty and submitted extensive written comments. I also thank Christopher A. Padilla, who supported Sam Palmisano on the Task Force, for his helpful advice and feedback.

We are thankful to several individuals who met with and briefed the Task Force group, including Commander of U.S. Cyber Command General Keith B. Alexander; White House cybersecurity coordinator J. Michael Daniel; U.S. Department of State coordinator for cyber issues Christopher M.E. Painter; U.S. Department of Commerce general counsel Cameron F. Kerry; National Telecommunications and Information Administration administrator Lawrence E. Strickling; Center for a New American Security president Richard Fontaine; and New America Foundation senior fellow Rebecca MacKinnon.

The report also benefited from a series of consultations with experts. Task Force member Bob Boorstin arranged a meeting with Eric Davis and Patrick Ryan at Google's Mountain View headquarters, and Task Force member Elliot J. Schrage organized a meeting with Facebook executives at their Menlo Park headquarters, as well as conference calls with Matt Perault and Sarah Wynn-Williams. Task Force member Peter

Cleveland also arranged meetings, in person and by phone, with David Hoffman and Audrey Plonk of Intel Corporation.

Thanks to CFR's National Program for organizing sessions with CFR members on the West Coast, including a roundtable at Microsoft in Seattle led by Task Force member Craig J. Mundie; a meeting in Menlo Park presided by CFR member Joseph Hurd; and a meeting in Los Angeles presided by Task Force member Ernest James Wilson III. And thanks to CFR's Corporate Program for organizing a dinner in Menlo Park with nineteen senior executives. Our thanks also go CFR's Meetings teams for organizing roundtables with CFR members in New York with Task Force members Elana Berkowitz and Eugene J. Huang, and in Washington, DC, with Task Force member Neal A. Pollard.

Our gratitude goes to CFR's Publications team for editing the report and readying it for publication. We extend additional thanks to CFR's various outreach departments, which have worked to ensure that the report reaches the widest audience possible.

Task Force Program Director Anya Schmemann and her teammates Kristin Lewis and Veronica Chiu were instrumental to this project from beginning to end, from the selection of Task Force members to the convening of meetings to the editing of drafts. I am indebted to them for their support and for keeping the project on track. My research associate Sharone Tobias and her predecessor, Patrick Browne, deserve credit and thanks for their research and assistance with the report. Former research associate Elizabeth Leader also provided support on several fronts.

I am grateful to CFR President Richard N. Haass and Director of Studies James M. Lindsay for giving me the opportunity to direct this effort. We thank the Markle Foundation for generously supporting this project.

Though this report is the product of the Independent Task Force, I take responsibility for its ultimate content and note that any omissions or mistakes are mine. Once again, my sincere thanks to all who contributed to this effort.

Adam M. Segal
Project Director

Acronyms

APEC	Asia-Pacific Economic Cooperation
ARPANET	Advanced Research Projects Agency Network
ASEAN	Association of Southeast Asian Nations
CFAA	Computer Fraud and Abuse Act
CISPA	Cyber Intelligence Sharing and Protection Act
CNCI	Comprehensive National Cybersecurity Initiative
DDoS	distributed denial of service
DHS	Department of Homeland Security
DNS	Domain Name System
DOD	Department of Defense
DOJ	Department of Justice
DOS	Department of State
EU	European Union
FBI	Federal Bureau of Investigation
GDP	gross domestic product
GGE	Groups of Governmental Experts
GNI	Global Network Initiative
GSP	Generalized System of Preferences
ICANN	Internet Corporation for Assigned Names and Numbers
ICS-CERT	Industrial Control Systems Cyber Emergency Response Team
ICT	information and communication technologies
IGF	Internet Governance Forum
IP	Internet Protocol

IPv4	Internet Protocol version 4
IPv6	Internet Protocol version 6
ISACs	Information Sharing and Analysis Centers
IT	information technology
ITRs	International Telecommunication Regulations
ITU	International Telecommunication Union
LulzSec	Lulz Security
MLAT	Mutual Legal Assistance Treaty
NATO	North Atlantic Trade Organization
NCCIC	National Cybersecurity and Communications Integration Center
NGO	nongovernmental organization
NIPP	National Infrastructure Protection Plan
NIST	National Institute of Standards and Technology
NSA	National Security Agency
NSC	National Security Council
OECD	Organization for Economic Cooperation and Development
OSCE	Organization for Security and Cooperation in Europe
PDD 63	Presidential Decision Directive 63
PIPA	PROTECT IP Act (Preventing Real Online Threats to Economic Creativity and Theft of Intellectual Property Act)
PSI	proliferation security initiative
R&D	research and development
SECURE IT	Strengthening and Enhancing Cybersecurity by Using Research, Education, Information, and Technology Act of 2012
SOPA	Stop Online Piracy Act
STEM	science, technology, engineering, and math
TLD	top-level domain
TPP	Trans-Pacific Partnership
TTIP	Transatlantic Trade and Investment Partnership

U.S.-CERT	U.S. Computer Emergency Readiness Team
USTR	U.S. Trade Representative
WCIT	World Conference on International Telecommunications
WTO	World Trade Organization

Task Force Report

Introduction: The Open and Global Internet Is Under Threat

Since the idea of a worldwide network was introduced in the early 1980s, the Internet has grown into a massive global system that connects over a third of the world's population, roughly 2.5 billion people. The Internet facilitates communication, commerce, trade, culture, research, and social and family connections and is now an integral part of modern life. Another 2.5 billion individuals are expected to get online by the end of this decade, mainly in the developing world, and further billions of devices and machines will be used. This enlargement to the rest of the globe could bring enormous economic, social, and political benefits to the United States and the world. New technologies could reshape approaches to disaster relief, diplomacy, conflict prevention, education, science, and cultural production.

However, as more people are connected in cyberspace and more critical services such as telecommunications, power, and transportation are interconnected, societies are becoming more dependent and more vulnerable to disruption. Escalating attacks on countries, companies, and individuals, as well as pervasive criminal activity, threaten the security and safety of the Internet. The number of high-profile, ostensibly state-backed operations continues to rise, and future attacks will become more sophisticated and disruptive. A global digital arms trade has now emerged that sells sophisticated malicious software to the highest bidders, including hacker tools and "zero-day exploits"—attacks that take advantage of previously unknown vulnerabilities.

U.S. government officials have increasingly warned of the danger of a massive, destructive attack, and the government and private sector are scrambling to prevent and prepare for future cyberattacks. *U.S. government warnings and efforts are important, but the United States should do more to prevent a potential catastrophic cyberattack. It also, in partnership with its friends and allies, must work to define the norms of cyberconflict.*

From its beginning, the Internet has been open and decentralized; its development and growth have been managed by a self-organizing, self-policing, and self-balancing collection of private and public actors. Today, as many countries seek increased security and control over the type of information and knowledge that flows across the Internet, that original vision is under attack. Some nation-states are seeking to fragment and divide the Internet and assert sovereignty over it; they are increasing their efforts to tightly regulate social, political, and economic activity and content in cyberspace and, in many cases, to suppress expression they view as threatening. At the December 2012 World Conference on International Telecommunications (WCIT), some countries moved to rewrite a 1988 treaty so that it sanctions government control of Internet technology and content. A truly global platform is being undermined by a collection of narrow national Internets.

For the past four decades, the United States was the predominant innovator, promoter, and shaper of cyberspace, but the window for U.S. leadership is now closing. In Asia, Latin America, and Africa, the number of networked users is rapidly increasing. Cyberspace is now becoming reflective of the world's Internet users. *The United States, with its friends and allies, needs to act quickly to encourage a global cyberspace that reflects shared values of free expression and free markets.*

Successfully meeting the challenges of the digital age requires a rethinking of domestic institutions and processes that were designed for the twentieth century. The rapid rate of technological change cannot help but outpace traditional legislative approaches and decision-making processes. The threats of the past were relatively slow developing and geographically rooted, so there was an appropriate distribution of authorities among defense, intelligence, law enforcement, and foreign policy agencies. Cyberattacks, however, can be launched from anywhere in the world, including from networks inside the United States, and their effects can be felt in minutes. Moreover, they do not always look like attacks. Many threats and actual compromises appear as little inconsistencies. Stolen data is not taken away, so the losses may never be noticed, but suddenly companies have new competitors or foreign actors have an uncanny insight into their enemies' activities.

In the United States, a lack of a coherent vision, the absence of appropriate authority to implement policy, and legislative gridlock are significant obstacles to global leadership. *The United States should act affirmatively to articulate norms of behavior, regulation, and partnership, or others will do so.* In addition, the effects of domestic decisions spread far beyond national borders and will affect not only users, companies, nongovernmental organizations (NGOs), and policymakers in other countries but also the health, stability, resilience, and integrity of the global Internet. *The bottom line is clear: digital foreign policy must begin with domestic policy.*

The opportunities for the United States in cyberspace are great, but a path needs to be found between a cyberspace that has no rules and one that permits governments to abuse their sovereignty. At the same time, policymakers have to realize that even the most successful digital policy will have limits to what it can accomplish. The United States' commitment to free speech, for example, is rooted in its history and culture, just as French and German attitudes are toward appropriate limits on online hate speech or the sale of Nazi paraphernalia. These differences are unlikely to completely disappear no matter how well policy is crafted.

To support security, innovation, growth, and the free flow of information, the Task Force recommends a U.S. digital policy based on four pillars:

- Alliances: The United States should help create a cyber alliance of like-minded actors—including governments, companies, NGOs, and the noncommercial sector—based on a common set of practices and principles.

- Trade: All future U.S. trade agreements should contain a goal of fostering the free flow of information and data across national borders while protecting intellectual property and developing an interoperable global regulatory framework for respecting the privacy rights of individuals.

- Governance: The United States should articulate and advocate a vision of Internet governance that includes emerging Internet powers and expands and strengthens the multi-stakeholder process.

- Security: U.S.-based industry should work more rapidly to develop a coherent industry-led approach to protect critical infrastructure from cyberattacks.

DEFENDING THE OPEN, GLOBAL INTERNET

Many of the benefits of cyberspace are self-reinforcing. Knowledge, information, and data cannot be shared across borders without some degree of security; an open and global Internet is likely to be more resilient than one that is fractured into multiple national intranets. Encouraging a healthy Internet ecosystem will preserve the Internet for future users. As a result, U.S. decision-makers do not have the luxury of pursuing Internet trade, freedom, and security policies in isolation.

In other instances, however, the demands for security, intellectual property protection, open access and innovation, privacy, and the free flow of information involve difficult trade-offs. Technologies that allow countries and companies to control and identify applications and content that pass through networks, for example, can increase security (and generate profit), but they can also cut against users' ability to develop new services and software. Technologies that ensure anonymity can be used by activists to oppose authoritarian regimes, but may also be abused by extremist groups. For example, in responding to the "Innocence of Muslims," the anti-Islam video made by a California resident and uploaded on YouTube, the State Department had to balance defending the U.S. tradition of free speech and condemning intolerance and hate speech, while acknowledging the legitimate fear of social media's power to quickly disseminate incendiary materials.

The year 2012 saw the battle over the Stop Online Piracy Act (SOPA) and Preventing Real Online Threats to Economic Creativity and Theft of Intellectual Property Act (PIPA). These two bills sought to make it harder for website operators—especially those outside the United States—to sell or distribute pirated copyrighted material or counterfeit goods. Though all sides in the debate agreed on the need to protect intellectual property from rogue foreign websites, technology companies, free speech activists, popular websites such as Wikipedia, and other critics argued that the provisions within the bills could result in the censorship of large quantities of noninfringing material, including political content, thereby severely limiting free expression and impairing future innovation.

These trade-offs and tensions are evident in foreign policy as well. One reason some users around the world support unconstrained access to the Internet is that it allows them to freely download (often pirated) entertainment. At the same time, autocrats are increasingly sophisticated about turning a blind eye to the piracy of movies and music but blocking political information. Any government effort to pursue a global anticensorship agenda and protect the intellectual property of U.S.-based companies must weigh these potential trade-offs.

The Task Force recognizes that there are both considerable opportunities and perilous challenges in cyberspace. This report identifies guiding principles and makes policy recommendations to mobilize a coalition of old friends and rising cyber powers, private firms, NGOs, and individual users to defend, reinforce, and expand an Internet that is open, global, secure, and resilient.

Now is the time for the United States, with its friends and allies, to ensure the Internet remains an open, global, secure, and resilient environment for users. Otherwise, many potential gains will be lost to political, economic, and strategic fighting over the shape of cyberspace.

Opportunities and Challenges of the Internet

The United States has benefited immensely from a digital infrastructure that is relatively open, global, secure, and resilient. The Internet is, in President Barack Obama's description, "the backbone that underpins a prosperous economy and a strong military and an open and efficient government."[1] The United States, however, will need to navigate through significant challenges in cyberspace, and the American vision of a free and open Internet is not shared by all. The economic, social, and political benefits of the Internet have been truly remarkable, but the next two decades could be even more transformational as cyberspace expands to more people and into more areas of activity. The cyber sphere presents great opportunities, but also significant challenges and dangers.

OPPORTUNITIES

Global Internet traffic is expected to triple over the next five years, with rapid growth in Africa, Latin America, and the Middle East. The world's Internet population nearly doubled between 2007 and 2013, and is now estimated at 2.27 billion people. The Cisco Visual Networking Index forecasts that by 2016 there will be 18.9 billion network connections, or almost 2.5 connections for each person on earth, compared with 10.6 billion in 2011. New products and services will be born as more devices are interconnected. Chips and sensors, smaller and more powerful, can be embedded in more products, creating vast amounts of data and linking physical and digital systems. The "Internet of things"—cars, ovens, office copiers, electrical grids, medical implants, and other Internet-connected machines that collect data and communicate—could result in thirty-one billion devices connected to the Internet in 2020.

Mobile services have penetrated almost all parts of the globe. Seventy-five percent of the world's population now has access to mobile phones, with five billion users located in developing countries. In countries within the Organization for Economic Cooperation and Development (OECD), wireless connections are the main source of recent Internet expansion, overtaking fixed broadband subscriptions in 2009. Furthermore, the developing world is more "mobile" than the developed; Africa is the fastest-growing mobile market in the world, with mobile accounting for approximately 90 percent of all telephone connections in northern Africa. Many innovations such as multi-SIM-card phones, low-value recharges, and mobile payments originated in less developed economies and diffused from there. This explosion of access to mobile phones, and mobile apps in particular, could lead to the creation of new markets and services, especially in agriculture, health, finance, and government.[2]

The United States continues to lead in information communication technology (ICT) funding at the national level, spending $1.2 trillion in 2010, compared with $487 billion in China, $385 billion in Japan, $200 billion in the United Kingdom (UK), and $66 billion in Russia.[3] Ranked by 2011 revenues, U.S. firms made up all of the top ten spenders in research and development (R&D) in information and communication technologies. Even with rising Asian ICT R&D levels, the United States still accounts for more than half of global ICT R&D and nearly all of the global growth in 2011 to 2012.[4]

The Internet economy accounted for 4.7 percent of U.S. gross domestic product (GDP) in 2010 ($68.2 billion), and is projected to rise to 5.4 percent of GDP in 2016. The United States captures more than 30 percent of global Internet revenues and more than 40 percent of net income.[5] Trade in content, media, and other intellectual property contributes $5 trillion and forty million jobs to the U.S. economy, according to the U.S. Department of Commerce.

The economic impact of the Internet is global. No widely accepted methodologies or metrics for assessing the full effect of the Internet on national economies exist yet, but it is estimated that for every 10 percent increase in broadband penetration, global GDP increases by an average of 1.3 percent. In a 2011 McKinsey study of thirteen countries (the G8 plus Brazil, South Korea, India, China, and Sweden), the Internet economy accounted for 3.4 percent of GDP and 7 percent of growth in these countries over the past fifteen years.[6] Measurement is even more difficult for developing economies, but early research suggests that increases in Internet penetration are associated with higher exports overall; increasing emerging-market mobile broadband penetration to more than 50 percent would yield returns of $420 billion and up to fourteen million jobs to the global economy.[7]

Limiting or shutting down the Internet has negative consequences. The OECD estimates that Egypt's decision to shut off the Internet for five days in January 2011 resulted in direct losses of $90 million, with indirect social and economic effects being much larger, perhaps reaching an additional $100 million.[8] In a March 2013 survey of 325 businesses with operations in China conducted by the American Chamber of Commerce in Beijing, 55 percent of the respondents said they saw China's Internet restrictions as negatively or somewhat negatively affecting their capacity to do business there.[9] Sixty-two percent said the disruption of foreign search engines make obtaining real-time market data, sharing time-sensitive information, or collaborating with colleagues based outside China more difficult; 72 percent responded that slow Internet speeds obstruct their ability to conduct business in China.

The Internet has also provided profound benefits to users that cannot be measured financially. Compared with radio, television, or other media, the Internet and mobile applications allow individuals to find and publish new information cheaply, quickly, and globally, thereby sharing knowledge and creating content. In many countries, Internet users are eroding the government monopoly control of mass media; these users can now report history for themselves and establish their own identities, real or fake.

Increasing access and connectivity will drive new abilities to provide education and deliver market information to isolated rural communities, monitor and respond to outbreaks of disease or natural disasters, and support increased citizen participation in political and social movements. M-Farm, for example, is a service that provides real-time price information to Kenyan farmers on mobile phones, allowing them to cut out middlemen and sell their produce at higher prices. After the 2010 earthquake, the Haitian government aggregated thousands of text messages about trapped victims that had been sent to an emergency text number. Volunteers translated them into English and plotted them on a crisis map for the U.S. Coast Guard. Twenty mobile applications developed by the state of Kerala in India have facilitated three million interactions between the government and its citizens since December 2010. Sixty-six percent of social media users in the United States—39 percent of all U.S. adults—have used social media to participate in politics by posting or responding to political views, following candidates, "liking" political content, or belonging to online groups.[10]

Within and across societies, the voices of individuals and communities have been strengthened, and government accountability and transparency have increased. The explosion of social media and communication technologies has added new tools to traditional diplomacy and also energized a new "government to society" diplomacy, allowing U.S. officials to communicate with more people in more places and to reach beyond governments.

Despite fears that the Internet and globalization more generally would lead to greater cultural homogeneity, cyberspace has been a platform for linguistic, artistic, cultural, religious, and ethnic expression. Examples include the growth in minority languages through the use of the Internet to connect diaspora communities. The use of Catalan online has grown substantially over the past ten years, connecting eight million speakers, and Catalan content has increased since the introduction of the top-level domain (TLD) name—.cat— in 2006. A TLD is at the highest level of the hierarchical Domain Name System (DNS), the designation .com, .org, .gov, and others that appears farthest to the right in an Internet address. Global Goods Partners, a nonprofit organization, is one of many websites that give artisans in developing countries a venue to sell traditional artwork and handicrafts to customers in developed countries.

The Internet has also allowed religious leaders and members to connect more easily. The Islamic Broadcasting Network, based in Washington, DC, broadcasts original programming on the Web to Muslim communities throughout the United States. Lakewood Church, based in Houston, Texas, is one of many churches that uses the Internet to reach out to parishioners and the general public: tens of thousands watch live-stream services, listen to podcasts, and read blog posts. Chabad.org, the website of the orthodox Jewish sect Lubavitch, claims 7.6 million visitors per month and 365,000 email subscribers.

The social and cultural innovation and economic growth powered by the Web are natural extensions of its structure. The Internet is the product of U.S. government-funded R&D, but it is now a global platform and the technical protocols underlying the networks were designed to allow decentralized and distributed growth. Without needing anyone's permission, an entrepreneur or activist can design hardware or software that runs on the network and individuals can create their own blogs or online businesses.

Many of the early Internet pioneers saw no need for the involvement of governments in cyberspace. They feared governments would restrict the rights to free expression and privacy, and so they developed a framework for the Internet based on self-regulation, private-sector leadership, and a bottom-up policy process.[11] Coordination of the core resources of the Internet—such as domain names, technical protocols, and root servers—emerged not from government dictate but as technical experts, businesses, civil society, and individual users formed organizations and associations to answer specific problems.

These organizations include representatives of the world's Internet users from governments, private industry, and civil society. For example, the Internet Engineering Task Force—an international group of leading technical experts concerned with the evolution of the Internet's architecture and smooth operation—endorses technical standards through an iterative "request for comment" process. The Internet Research Task Force promotes long-term research on Internet protocols, applications, architecture, and technology. Governments, business, and civil society can debate governance issues at the Internet Governance Forum. On the technical side is the Internet Corporation for Assigned Names and Numbers (ICANN), which was created in 1998 as a U.S.-based, private nonprofit corporation and subsequently signed a contract with the U.S. Department of Commerce to take over a variety of oversight tasks. ICANN now coordinates Internet Protocol (IP) addresses, the numerical sequence that serves as an identifier for an Internet server; the Domain Name System, which allows users to refer to websites using easier-to-remember domain names rather than the all-numeric IP addresses; and the root server system, the master list of all top-level domain names.

Few would credit these groups with a perfect record, but they have managed—working without government regulation—to reflect a broad range of perspectives and keep pace with rapidly changing technology. They have helped shape a free and open environment in which the Internet adapts to change, generates tremendous economic growth, and fosters innovation.

CHALLENGES

The open, global Internet is unlikely to continue to flourish without deliberate action to promote and defend it. Political, economic, and technological forces are seeking to splinter the Internet into something that looks more like national networks, with each government controlling its domestic sphere as well as the flow of data and information between countries. *A global Internet increasingly fragmented into national Internets is not in the interest of the United States.*

Justifying their actions by claiming they are protecting children or national security, more than forty governments have erected restrictions of information, data, and knowledge flow on the Internet or blocked access to sites through other means. Iran, for example, has blocked Twitter and YouTube and has announced that all Internet users will be forced to use a new system created and restricted by the Iranian government. A November 2012 law in Russia created a blacklist of websites that is purported to limit access to sites that promote suicide and illegal drug use, but has also affected political and social groups. These restrictions create barriers to the transfer of knowledge among societies and run counter to the concept of a free and open Internet.

Serious differences over whether and how to restrict access to certain types of information in cyberspace exist even among multiparty, multiethnic democracies. The European Human Rights Commission, for example, identifies a "margin of appreciation"—an acceptance that some states, depending on cultural or historic traditions, may restrict speech and political activity to some degree in order to protect public morals. At the same time, the European Court of Human Rights has ruled that the Turkish government violated human rights when it completely banned YouTube from March 2007 to October 2010. In January 2013, a Paris court ordered Twitter to identify the authors of anti-Semitic tweets and create a mechanism to alert French authorities to "illegal content." British officials called for BlackBerry Messenger to be shut off during riots in August 2011, and San Francisco Bay Area Rapid Transit authorities turned off wireless networks in stations to disrupt protests. Brazil detained a Google executive when the company refused to take down videos that criticized a candidate in a mayoral election, releasing the executive only when the company complied with the order. India has restricted the number of text messages it allows users to send during outbreaks of communal violence and asked Twitter, Facebook, and Google to censor sensitive and blasphemous posts. In Thailand, broad application of lèse-majesté—laws against insulting or defaming the monarchy—and the Computer Crimes Act have resulted in the restriction of videos on YouTube and long prison sentences for bloggers and activists.

Various nations—China, Russia, Iran, Pakistan, and Saudi Arabia among them—want to extend national sovereignty into cyberspace and are pushing for a more state-centric system to manage the Internet. These countries have pursued these goals for many years, but the competing visions came to a head in Dubai in December 2012 at the International Telecommunication Union's (ITU) World Conference on International Telecommunications. In the run-up to the meeting, the United States and its allies argued that the Internet should remain outside the regulation of the ITU and did not belong in the International Telecommunication Regulations (ITRs). When that argument failed, the United States rejected the rewritten ITRs, opposing provisions on network security, control of spam, the International Telecommunication Union's role in Internet governance, and the definitions of authorities and actors that would have threatened the multi-stakeholder model of the Internet and provided justification to states that want to increase their surveillance of the Web. The language detailing how cybersecurity measures would be implemented, for example, was broad enough to allow for an abuse of power by states claiming to fight cyber criminals but actually cracking down on dissidents.

Fifty-four other countries joined the United States, but another eighty-nine signed the document. Some of the signatories are authoritarian regimes that fear the free flow of information and are happy to paint Washington's opposition to the ITU as self-serving, designed to protect U.S. influence and the market position of American technology companies. Yet a significant number that signed did so because they lack cybersecurity or other technical expertise, have a long history of dealing with the ITU, and see it as a credible partner. Many of the African countries that signed the treaty, for example, needed help in alleviating undeserved charges that mobile phone users incur when receiving unwanted spam messages on their phones.

Feeling shut out of the bottom-up model of Internet governance, the same states may have little appreciation of the benefits of the process. They may not have had close contact with any of the institutions of the multi-stakeholder model. NGOs, especially in the developing world, often lack the resources to travel to meetings to participate in relevant processes. In addition, some nations have voiced complaints about their experiences with the multi-stakeholder model. ICANN's four-year delay in rolling out new international (as opposed to generic) top-level domain names, for example, alienated many in the developing world.[12]

The ITRs bind only those that sign them, and so the refusal by the United States and its allies created two tiers of treaty status, with the United States and abstaining countries remaining on the 1988 ITRs. Nevertheless, the division between those nations committed to an open, free Internet and those that believe governments should monopolize control of the Internet did not first surface at the WCIT. It has, however, been a running battle for at least a decade and emerged again in May 2013 at the fifth meeting of ITU's World Telecommunication/ICT Policy Forum and at the World Summit on the Information Society.[13] In addition, the ITU has organized study groups to redefine its regulatory role in areas such as cloud computing, mobile, and next-generation networks. In 2014, the ITU plenipotentiary meeting will define the group's mission, rewrite its constitution, and elect a new secretary-general. Currently, no candidate for the position is committed to the multi-stakeholder process.

Restrictive and discriminatory operating rules complicate trade and slow global economic growth. Filtering, blocking, and other limitations on data flow make it more difficult for companies to reach their customers and provide services or critical information to be shared globally. Governments are also erecting new regulatory barriers to cross-border, information-driven businesses. Brunei and Vietnam, for example, have data residency laws requiring companies to store the data they collect only on in-country servers; such regulations could seriously undermine the efficiency of cloud computing—the delivery of data and other services over the Internet—and shut out foreign companies from domestic markets. A number of other states are also either considering or have proposed regulations that require payment processing systems be located within their territories, which would have a similar dampening effect on global businesses.

Moreover, regulations that constrict the flow of information not only create disparities among people's access to knowledge but also have a negative effect on the shape, architecture, safety, and resilience of the Internet. In 2012, for example, two proposals in the U.S. Congress to allow for filtering of the DNS, which would enable the government to require U.S. companies to block access to certain websites, posed a significant risk to a wider cybersecurity strategy.[14]

Administrative and technological changes over the next few years threaten to destabilize the current bottom-up approach to governance that combines the private and nonprofit sectors. The expansion of the DNS, for example, is intended to enhance competition, innovation, and consumer choice, but critics fear that without adequate coordination and oversight it could instead create consumer confusion, undermine copyright and brand rights, and increase the opportunity for cyber crime.[15] For example, while many of the new generic top-level domains (e.g., .app, .search, .cloud, .news, etc.) will be managed by government entities, municipalities, standards bodies, and nonprofits, others will be managed by private companies who may be tempted to act as profit-motivated gatekeepers furthering their own private interests, rather than as stewards of the public interest managing a public resource.

Furthermore, the original pool of Internet Protocol version 4 (IPv4) addresses has nearly been exhausted. When IPv4 was developed in the late 1970s, it was hard to imagine that the world would need more than four billion unique IP addresses. But with the expansion of Internet use around the world, and the explosive growth of broadband services and mobile devices, there will soon not be enough addresses for everyone (or thing) that requests one. The new technological standard, Internet Protocol version 6 (IPv6), will provide 340 undecillion addresses, but deployment has been slow and unsteady.[16] The new standard is not immediately interoperable with the old, and switching imposes real costs on Internet service providers. Some of the programs used to translate between the two standards degrade performance, and Asia is adopting IPv6 at much faster rates; uneven deployment will have a negative impact on overall performance.

CYBER CRIME AND CYBER ECONOMIC ESPIONAGE

A divided cyberspace is a less than ideal result for the United States, but the future could be even more anarchic. Escalating attacks are challenging the defenses of even the most sophisticated banks and institutions. In September and October 2012, January 2013, and again in March 2013, cyberattacks disrupted the websites of Wells Fargo, J.P. Morgan Chase,

Citigroup, U.S. Bancorp, PNC Financial Services, American Express, and Bank of America. The attacks did no damage to customer information or the companies' computer networks, but were unusually large and used infected servers in data centers around the world. Although a hacker group calling itself Izz ad-Din al-Qassam Cyber Fighters took credit for the attacks, U.S. officials have argued that the attacks originated in Iran or, at the least, were tolerated by Iranian officials. The networks of South Korea's three major banks and two largest broadcasters were disrupted in March 2013, possibly by North Korean hackers, during a time of escalating military tension on the peninsula.

To date, the effects of the attacks have been primarily economic, and the estimates of the costs of cyber crime vary widely. Symantec Corporation estimates a cost to consumers of $110 billion globally, and a PricewaterhouseCoopers report claims a cost of $500 billion in 2011. One of the first academic studies, however, of direct, indirect, and defense costs for credit card fraud, online banking fraud, fake antivirus, and other scams reported a significantly smaller total of just under $25 billion.[17]

Cyber economic espionage targets companies' business strategies, intellectual property, and the products of expensive, decades-long R&D projects, thus eroding their competitive economic advantage. General Keith Alexander, head of the U.S. National Security Agency (NSA) and U.S. Cyber Command, has called cyber economic espionage attacks on American companies the "greatest transfer of wealth in history," and estimates that American companies have lost $250 billion in stolen information and another $114 billion in related expenses.[18] Furthermore, these attacks are accelerating, increasing by 75 percent between 2011 and 2012, according to the Defense Security Service.[19] Companies, however, for various legal and economic reasons, are hesitant to discuss these attacks publicly. The twenty-seven largest U.S. companies reporting cyberattacks, for example, say they sustained no major financial losses.[20]

DISRUPTIVE AND POLITICAL ATTACKS

Other attacks have been disruptive and political. In March 2013, Cyberbunker, a Dutch company that hosts a website said to be sending spam, launched a record distributed denial of service (DDoS) attack on Spamhaus, a volunteer spam filtering organization. A DDoS attack is the use of multiple compromised computers to flood a target with data in an effort to knock it offline. In this case, the attack spread to multiple Internet exchanges and ultimately slowed down traffic for users—primarily in Europe, but also in the Middle East, Africa, and Asia-Pacific.[21] Activist hacker groups such as Anonymous and Lulz Security (LulzSec) have targeted government agencies, international organizations, and multinational corporations. Political hacking, website defacement, and DDoS attacks are now a common part of political conflict and even war, as seen in some examples from the Middle East and Asia. China-based hackers have apparently conducted cyber espionage campaigns against civil society actors, exile organizations, political movements, individual dissidents, think tanks, and media outlets such as the *New York Times*, *Wall Street Journal*, Bloomberg, and *Washington Post*.

Governments have found cyberattacks to be a useful political and military tool, and state-backed attackers were apparently behind Flame, malware that stole information from thousands of computers in the Middle East; Duqu, a worm that spies on industrial control systems; Stuxnet, malware designed to cripple Iran's nuclear centrifuges; Shamoon, malware that struck Saudi Aramco and destroyed data on approximately thirty thousand computers; and Red October, malware that targets Russian language documents in Eastern European and Central Asian countries. Experts estimate that approximately forty countries have or are acquiring cyber weapons for use in combat.[22] Former U.S. secretary of defense Leon Panetta has warned that governments or extremist groups could use cyber tools to gain control of critical industrial control systems and launch attacks on critical U.S. infrastructure, producing widespread destruction equivalent to a "cyber Pearl Harbor."[23] Hackers could remotely modify or reprogram industrial control systems that control pipelines, train tracks, dams, and electricity networks, destroying machinery and creating physical damage and destruction. In 2011, the Department of Homeland Security (DHS) reported a 383 percent increase in attacks on critical infrastructure.[24]

The vivid claim of a "cyber Pearl Harbor" may raise awareness and focus policy attention, but the Task Force finds that the most pressing current threat is not likely to be a single, sudden attack that cripples the United States. Such attacks involve elaborate intelligence preparation, great uncertainty for the attacker, and are subject to some level of deterrence through interdependence in the case of major states like China.[25] *Rather, the Task Force finds that the more likely threat is a proliferation of attacks that steal strategically important or valuable data and destroy confidence in the safety and trustworthiness of the Internet.* These less-elaborate attacks involve less preparation, but can nevertheless do great damage to the confidence that makes modern banking, transport, and communications systems work. Over time, however, future attacks could become even more destructive as cyber weapons and capacities proliferate and as electricity, power, transport, and communications infrastructures become increasingly dependent on the Internet. The barriers to entry are low on cyberattack tools, unlike nuclear weapons, and individuals with limited experience can quickly become capable of conducting disruptive actions in cyberspace.

Cyberspace could also become much more Orwellian. Technologies that allow for greater geolocation of users and inspection of data may improve security by making it much harder to attack anonymously, but also may reduce the innovative or generative capacities of the Internet. The plummeting cost of data storage and collection, as well as the proliferation of surveillance and biometric technologies, could strengthen authoritarian regimes and severely hamper the ability of individuals to organize, spread information and knowledge, and protest.

Current U.S. Policy:
Continuity and Growth

Policymakers have continually struggled with the challenges of the digital age. Cyberspace crosses the borders between government agencies, the public and private sectors, and nations, forcing all actors into new, often uncomfortable relationships and strained cooperation. In addition, most policymakers are neither technically knowledgeable nor culturally attuned to the ethos of the digital era. The Internet works in large part because it is self-organizing, self-policing, and self-balancing. Thus, a degree of humility about the extent to which policymakers can prevent the most deleterious outcomes and shape the future is in order.

Policy decisions need to respond to and channel the economic and technological forces that are going to drive the evolution of cyberspace. Although a U.S. government initiative, Advanced Research Projects Agency Network (ARPANET), kick-started the cyber age, the growth of these global networks has been determined largely by private and commercial forces. The networks that support this platform are distributed by and into private hands, and it is technology companies and individual end users that will innovate the next generation of technologies. Private industry, however, does not speak with one voice. The entertainment industry and technology companies, for example, have significant differences in attitudes toward Internet regulation and the protection of intellectual property.

Many of the fundamental tenets of U.S. strategy toward cyberspace—private sector in the lead, public-private partnerships, information sharing, international outreach—emerged in the 1990s. In 1998, the Clinton administration released *A Framework for Global Electronic Commerce*, which called for the private sector to take the lead in the development of the Internet and for government to avoid imposing unnecessary restrictions. A white paper that same year called for movement of the DNS from the federal government to a private, nonprofit, internationally representative organization eventually known as the Internet Corporation for Assigned Names and Numbers, or ICANN. Presidential Decision Directive 63 (PDD 63), the first national cybersecurity strategy, was released in May 1998 and focused on critical infrastructure protection and public-private partnerships, and it created several information-sharing organizations such as the Information Sharing and Analysis Centers and National Infrastructure Protection Center. Later that same year, the Pentagon established the first joint cyber war fighting group, the Joint Task Force for Computer Network Defense.

The 2003 *National Strategy to Secure Cyberspace* also concentrated on defending critical infrastructure, echoing the calls for private leadership and better public-private coordination of the preceding policies: "In general, the private sector is best equipped and structured to respond to an evolving cyber threat."[26] The strategy called for the government to work with private industry to create an emergency response system to cyberattacks, as well as measures for strengthening counterintelligence, improving attack attribution, and using international organizations to facilitate a "global 'culture of security.'" In the last days of his administration, President George W. Bush launched the Comprehensive National Cybersecurity Initiative (CNCI).[27] CNCI called for the development of an intrusion detection system and designated DHS to play the lead role in defending government networks, the implementation of a government-wide cyber counterintelligence plan, development of deterrence strategies, and the definition of the federal government's role for extending cybersecurity into critical infrastructure.

CYBERSPACE AND THE OBAMA ADMINISTRATION

The Obama administration signaled the importance of cybersecurity early in its first term. In February 2009, President Obama ordered a sixty-day review of cybersecurity plans and programs.[28] The review noted that the nation was at a crossroads of maintaining a digital infrastructure that encourages efficiency and innovation, and protecting safety, security, and privacy. It recognized that the private sector "designs, builds, owns, and operates most of the digital infrastructure," but that the federal government "cannot entirely delegate or abrogate its role in securing the nation from a cyber incident or accident." The review recommended the appointment of a cyber policy coordinator, dual-hatted to the National Security Council (NSC) and National Economic Council; evaluation and continuation of much of the Comprehensive National Cybersecurity Initiative; and designation of a privacy and civil liberties official to the NSC cybersecurity directorate. As the administration reportedly had difficulty finding a suitable candidate for the position, much of the attention in the first year after the review focused on whether the cyber "czar" would have the appropriate budget, access to the president, and political authority necessary to coordinate the numerous agencies responsible for cyberspace. These questions remain today.

The Obama administration review also called for development of an international cybersecurity policy framework, which was released two years later, in May 2011. The *International Strategy for Cyberspace* laid out an overarching vision of the agenda for cyberspace: protecting freedom of expression, promoting innovation and protecting intellectual property, supporting the multi-stakeholder model, preventing attacks and crime, and enabling military operations. The strategy identifies the use of diplomacy, defense, and development "to promote an open, interoperable, secure, and reliable information and communications infrastructure."[29] The diplomatic process is to mirror the processes of the Internet itself—"distributed systems require distributed action"— and so U.S. diplomats have engaged with multiple actors in multiple forums: close partners and NATO; the G8 and regional groupings such as the Association of Southeast Asian Nations (ASEAN) Regional Forum and the Organization for Security and Cooperation in Europe (OSCE); the United Nations and the ITU; and technical and other working groups. In addition, the strategy has a deterrence component, clearly stating that the United States "will respond to hostile acts in cyberspace as we would to any other threat to our country." The U.S. response will not necessarily be limited to cyber, but may also include diplomatic, informational, military, and economic means.

The strategy called for U.S. officials to concentrate their efforts in eight areas: international standards and open markets, network defense, military alliances and cooperative security, Internet governance, international development and capacity building, the support of Internet freedom and privacy, law enforcement, and extending the reach of the Council of Europe's Convention on Cybercrime (also known as the Budapest Convention). The convention establishes a baseline set of laws; parties to the treaty agree to criminalize computer crimes, including illegal access and interception, data and system interference, misuse of devices, forgery, fraud, child pornography, and intellectual property offenses. It also requires signatories to cooperate in the investigation and prosecution of crimes, though states can opt out of the duty to cooperate if the request infringes on sovereignty, security, or other critical interests. As of March 2013, thirty-nine countries have ratified the treaty, including the United States, but China and Russia are among the scores of countries that have not signed.[30] Russia has protested against a provision in the treaty that would let foreign investigators work directly with network operators and avoid government officials, while other nation-states have complained they were not part of the convention's creation or are skeptical of the convention's European provenance.

In May 2010, the United States created U.S. Cyber Command, and deterrence and other military components of cyberspace were further developed in the 2011 Department of Defense (DOD) *Strategy for Operating in Cyberspace*. The strategy has five components: treat cyberspace as an operational domain—in addition to land, sea, air, and space—to organize, train, and equip so that DOD can take full advantage of cyberspace's potential; develop the concept of *active defense*; partner with the public and private sectors; leverage talent and innovation; and work with U.S. allies and partners to build new cybersecurity relationships.[31] Notably absent, however, was a discussion of offensive cyber operations, for which DOD has developed some classified doctrine and rules of engagement, according to press reports. At his confirmation hearing, Secretary of State John Kerry called cyberattacks a "twenty-first century nuclear weapons equivalent," and pledged to engage in diplomacy and negotiation to establish rules of the road for cyberspace.

In three speeches over 2010 and 2011, former secretary of state Hillary Clinton laid out the opportunities arising from and threats to the free flow of information on the Internet.[32] Clinton identified information networks as a "new nervous system for our planet" and asserted that users must be assured freedom of expression and religion online, as well as the right to access the Internet and thereby connect to websites and other people. The State Department has promoted these four freedoms in international organizations and funded the development of technologies to allow users to circumvent censorship and remain safe online. Officials have also collaborated with grassroots organizations around the world to help them use online tools and develop strategies to magnify their influence. The Internet Freedom Fellows program, for example, brings human rights activists to Geneva, Washington, and Silicon Valley to meet with other advocates, U.S. and international government leaders, and members of civil society and the private sector.[33] Clinton also called on private-sector companies to do more to protect the flow of information both by resisting calls for censorship from countries they do business in and by restricting sales of hardware, software, and technology services that could be abused by authoritarian regimes. The State Department under John Kerry is expected to make an even more aggressive push in using the tools of social networking in public diplomacy in order to communicate with citizens in critical countries and regions.

Parallel to these security and diplomatic efforts, the Commerce Department's Internet Policy Task Force has been conducting a "comprehensive review of the nexus between privacy policy, copyright, global free flow of information, cybersecurity, and innovation in the Internet economy."[34] Work in the area of privacy is most developed and is expected to serve as a template for the other areas. The basic assumption is that regulation is necessary to maintain consumer trust, but should remain light to promote innovation and growth. For example, the Consumer Bill of Rights is not prescriptive but a code of conduct developed in cooperation with industry and civil society, which could become legally enforceable. The Department of Commerce is also working with the Asia-Pacific Economic Cooperation (APEC) forum and the European Union (EU) so U.S. standards on privacy are interoperable with global practices. In addition, Commerce and the U.S. Trade Representative (USTR) should also support other nations' efforts to protect intellectual property and protect against illegal piracy of copyrighted works.

GUIDING PRINCIPLES: THE UNITED STATES SHOULD GET ITS HOUSE IN ORDER AND WORK WITH PARTNERS

More than any of its predecessors, the Obama administration has developed a comprehensive and energetic strategy for cyberspace. But for the United States to build on these policy efforts, it needs to get its domestic house in order. Given its historic role in developing the Internet and because U.S. companies and universities remain at the technological cutting edge, the United States continues to be an important role model, both positively and negatively. Washington's influence is more likely to be positive when it recognizes cyberspace is a global issue, not one simply of national economic, strategic, and political interest. Previous success in areas such as democracy promotion and human rights depended heavily on leadership by example. *If the United States wants to lead in cyberspace, it should practice what it preaches.*

The lack of U.S. coordination and coherent vision and the absence of appropriate authority to implement policy are important barriers to global leadership for the United States. Cyberspace policymaking is spread primarily among the White House and the Departments of Defense, State (DOS), Commerce, Justice (DOJ), and Homeland Security; no single individual or agency is in charge, short of the president. Decentralizing the process has advantages, but the White House needs to better define national roles, strategies, and responsibilities, especially among the trio of DOD, DHS, and DOJ.

The erratic and somewhat desultory debate on domestic regulatory standards for cybersecurity risks ceding the initiative to more active parties, especially the European Union. This may happen even without the EU actively imposing or other states willingly adopting European standards. In a number of economic sectors, regulations have migrated from Brussels to other economies in part because of market size and the EU capability, as well as the prohibitive cost to firms of maintaining different standards in different markets.[35]

The United States should be cognizant that its actions at home reverberate abroad. The State and Commerce Departments, for example, promote ICANN's role in the multi-stakeholder model of Internet governance as counter to the ITU. Many states are already skeptical of ICANN's autonomy from U.S. government control, given its history and the Commerce Department's contract with ICANN. Congressional efforts to pressure the Commerce Department to have ICANN respond to demands outside of the usual consultative process undermine executive branch efforts to make ICANN more of an independent, truly global, and representative policy authority.[36]

When the United States works counter to its principles and restricts cyberspace, it provides justification and coverage to other states looking to limit the openness of the Internet. Other countries act based upon what the United States does rather than what it says. Beijing and Moscow often argue that their efforts to control the free flow of information are no different than those of Washington, Paris, or Berlin to block access to pirated materials or limit offensive speech. Censorship, blocking, and filtering may generate reactions from actors that may create unknown outcomes or actually worsen the health, security, and resilience of the Internet.[37]

The United States should do more to engage other states in cyberspace. Cybersecurity cooperation and collaboration is being expanded among the Five Eyes (the Technical Cooperation Program composed of Australia, Canada, New Zealand, the United Kingdom, and the United States); the United States and Australia have declared that their mutual defense treaty applies to cyberattacks; and the United States, through integrated government agency participation or a "whole-of-government" approach, has begun to hold cyber bilateral meetings with India, Brazil, South Africa, South Korea, Japan, and Germany that include representatives from the Departments of Defense, State, Commerce, Justice, and Homeland Security. The United States is also working with its negotiating partners to make sure that the forthcoming Trans-Pacific Partnership (TPP) trade agreement codifies the free flow of information across national boundaries.

The United States has also had success in promoting the free flow of information and knowledge both by appealing to established national and international norms and by working in tandem with and sometimes ceding the lead to other countries. For example, in 2011, the Netherlands organized a meeting of governments to stand up for free expression on the Internet. The eighteen governments that make up the Freedom Online Coalition are often able to conduct discussions without provoking the same level of suspicion and opposition that the United States alone has to overcome.[38]

This traditional state-to-state diplomacy is necessary, but nowhere near sufficient for cyberspace. Righting domestic policy is important, but the United States cannot go it alone. *It is necessary for the United States to identify partners among governments, the business community, and civil society at home and abroad.* Sharing leadership in cyberspace is essential if the United States is to maintain and improve what it has helped to build.

Numerous civil actors such as the Global Network Initiative, Open-Net Initiative, Electronic Frontier Foundation, and the Center for Democracy and Technology advocate for openness and human rights on the Internet. Close coordination with Sweden and the Netherlands on efforts to promote the right to connect work in tandem with the U.S. State Department getting circumvention tools in the hands of individual users and running "tech camps" for NGOs around the world. Similarly, any effort to develop rules, institutions, and norms for cybersecurity should involve private companies, international law enforcement, and international legal experts.

Recommendations: The United States and Its Partners Should Promote a Positive Agenda for Cyberspace

For at least two decades, it has been clear that the U.S. government has been unable to keep up with the pace of technological change. Moore's law purports that many of the capacities of digital technology double every two years. But, with procurement processes that can require eighteen to twenty-four months, the government is always chasing the next wave and operating with outdated equipment.[39] Moreover, today's threats compress time and ignore geography in ways that overtax the capacities of even the best institutions. In the past, most threats could be seen over the horizon, across national borders, and prepared for over weeks, months, or years. By contrast, cyberattacks ignore territorial boundaries and can be indistinct from criminal activity. Attackers can be inside U.S. networks in minutes, if not seconds. Given the speed of cyberattacks, thoughtful deliberation during an event may be difficult, if not impossible; much of the response to cyber events will be automated, requiring the pre-positioning of resources and authority.

It is not just conflict that is accelerated. Previously, countries with rising economies developed advanced scientific and research capabilities over a span of decades. Now, countries that want to move up the value chain can steal the results of years of research and development and billions of dollars' worth of intellectual property from their trading partners in a matter of hours.

Successfully meeting the challenges of the digital age requires an expansive and far-reaching rethinking of institutions and processes designed for the twentieth century. The authorities given to the Department of Justice, the Department of Defense, and the intelligence communities in the Title 10, 18, and 50 codes, for example, were developed when threats materialized over time and there was a clearer distinction between external and internal threats and criminal and military activity. Other countries, moreover, are not constrained by such distinctions. *U.S. policymakers need to fix the disconnect between existing capabilities and jurisdiction and determine how best to reform and remake government agencies.*

For the near term, the Task Force identifies the following foreign and trade policies in the areas of security and resilience, trade, and governance.

SECURITY AND RESILIENCE

As part of the effort to help build a safe and resilient Internet ecosystem, the Task Force recommends the following:

- The United States should help create a cyber alliance of like-minded actors—including governments, companies, NGOs, and the non-commercial sector—based on a common set of practices and principles.

- The United States—first with its allies and then with other states—should adopt a whole-of-government approach that involves integrated government agency participation to limit the exposure of industrial control systems to damaging attacks and controlling the growing market in and proliferation of cyber weapons.

- The State Department and the Justice Department should work with like-minded nations to build an International Cyber Crime Center.

- Senior U.S. government officials should adopt a greater degree of transparency about the potential offensive use of cyber weapons.

- The State and Defense Departments should secure the cooperation of other states, civil society groups, and international legal experts, especially from the developing world, to clarify and expand the acceptance of the laws of armed conflict to the cyber domain.

- The United States should develop a strategy to counter cyber economic espionage that includes incorporating the prohibition against economic cyber espionage in multilateral and bilateral agreements, as well as directing national security resources to identify and collect intelligence on foreign efforts to target specific U.S. companies.

- Congress should consider amending statutes such as the Computer Fraud and Abuse Act so the private sector has greater certainty about whether it can take active defense and more offensive-oriented actions in cyberspace to protect its property.

- The U.S. government should recruit, train, and retain a specialized cyber service.

- Congress should pass sensible cybersecurity legislation that allows for the rapid sharing of threat information.

- The White House should strengthen the coordinating authority of the National Cybersecurity and Communications Integration Center, as well as increase the authority of cyber policymakers across the government.

CREATE A CYBER ALLIANCE

During the Cold War, the United States signaled its commitment to and built security cooperation through the North Atlantic Trade Organization (NATO) and other alliance agreements. Within NATO, the member countries are committed to a mutual self-defense agreement that treats an attack on one by an external party as an attack on the group. NATO has few forces of its own, but it does have an integrated military structure to field and command member-country forces once they agree to a NATO-related mission. NATO is also a political alliance, promoting democratic values and shared interests and partnering with other nations and international organizations, such as Japan and South Korea, and the United Nations.

Washington should build a cyber alliance, a coalition of like-minded actors—including governments, companies, and NGOs—based on a common set of Internet practices and principles. This should happen at multiple levels with different sets of actors. The result should be a number of flexible groupings linked together in a consortium for an open, global, secure, and resilient Internet.

The United States already has growing commitments to its allies and partners in cybersecurity. NATO has agreed to include cyber in the defense planning process; provide coordinated assistance if an ally or allies are victims of a cyberattack; develop early warning, situational awareness, and analysis capabilities; and help members achieve a minimum level of defense and reduce vulnerabilities of national critical infrastructures.[40] The Australia, New Zealand, and United States Security Treaty (New Zealand is an inactive member) has been extended to cover cyberattacks, and a substantial attack could trigger the use of the alliance to allow for technical cooperation among the countries.

But there are opportunities for greater leadership. Other nations are looking to Washington to do more diplomatically to better coordinate and integrate cyber defense. The Defense Department should expand military-to-military contact and training of civilian and defense authorities, conduct joint cyber exercises, develop a common set of security practices and technology standards, and share data on threats and remediation. The Pentagon and the State Department should also continue to work with close friends and partners to offer technical assistance to less-developed countries.

First with its allies and then with other states, the United States should cooperate on limiting the exposure of industrial control systems to damaging attacks and controlling the growing market in and proliferation of cyber weapons.[41] These types of discussions are sensitive and probably classified, but frank discussions are needed to extract best practices and identify mutual threats. The Department of Homeland Security should expand engagement with foreign counterparts in discussions on the capabilities of terrorist groups, as well as best practices for security in the oil, chemical, energy, and telecommunications sectors. Intelligence and law enforcement agencies should look for more aggressive ways to find and shut down the online black markets that proliferate malware that could harm industrial control systems. The United States has a long history of such intelligence sharing and cooperation with foreign partners, even on sensitive matters when interests align, such as has been the case in combating terrorism.

With other like-minded states, the United States should address the problem of sanctuary states—territories unwilling or unable to rein in cyber crime. Beyond the positive economic impact and improvement in public trust that a reduction in theft would bring, it would also filter out some of the background noise for state-backed cyber espionage or other attacks. Criminal and espionage networks are converging, with spies and criminals sharing methods, targets, and exploits.

As noted earlier, the State Department has promoted the Budapest Convention on Cyber Crime as a mechanism for addressing international crime. The convention is a useful process, and a number of countries, including Japan and Australia, have recently ratified the treaty. Still, it appears unlikely that the convention's norms will be globally accepted, especially as Russia, China, and other important economic actors remain outside of the convention. With its partners, the United

States should increase both public pressure and offers of technical assistance to police and incident response teams.

The State Department and Justice Department should work with like-minded nations to build an International Cyber Crime Center that focuses on solving crimes and achieving successful prosecutions and to expand existing mechanisms, such as INTERPOL, that focus on apprehending cyber and traditional criminals.[42] Member states could also complain to the center when they feel that they have not received adequate assistance from other governments. The center would publicly name and pressure states that give sanctuary to cyber criminals and provide a grievance procedure for members that felt they did not receive adequate assistance from other governments. The center would also work alongside the INTERPOL Global Complex for Innovation, which will open in Singapore in 2014.[43] The complex will function as an R&D lab, training facility, and forensics lab for cyber crime.

A cyber alliance needs to be expansive, embracing more than state-to-state diplomacy and involving private companies, international law enforcement, and NGOs. For instance, the Conficker Working Group, a coalition of public and private cybersecurity organizations, companies, and researchers, worked to prevent the spread of a computer worm and block the infected computers from receiving updates and commands. The Federal Bureau of Investigation (FBI), Facebook, and law enforcement agencies in Bosnia and Herzegovina, Croatia, Britain, New Zealand, and Peru cooperated to dismantle the Butterfly botnet, a collection of compromised computers controlled by a third party.

In the case of DDoS attacks, private companies, civil society groups, and governments can increase resilience through mutual aid agreements. Website operators, for example, can link and mirror other third-party sites. If the third-party site goes down, other sites can show users' stored versions of what was on the attacked site.[44] The Department of Homeland Security should also offer grants and prizes to technology or business groups that help colleagues to mitigate intrusions and DDoS attacks.

In sum, the United States needs to be willing to work with a range of actors that can help build, protect, and maintain a safe operating environment. The World Economic Forum, for example, is promoting the Principles for Cyber Resilience through global partnerships with public and private actors. Signatories of the principles commit themselves not only to raising their ability to protect digital assets but also to protect others.[45]

SUMMARY OF RECOMMENDATIONS

- Washington should build a cyber alliance, a coalition of like-minded actors based on a common set of Internet practices and principles.

- The Defense Department should expand military-to-military contact and training of civilian and defense authorities, conduct joint cyber exercises, and share data on threats and remediation.

- The Department of Homeland Security should expand engagement with foreign counterparts in discussions on the capabilities of terrorist groups, as well as best practices for security in the oil, chemical, energy, and telecommunications sectors.

- Intelligence and law enforcement agencies should look for more aggressive ways to find and shut down the online black markets that proliferate malware that could harm industrial control systems.

- The State Department and Justice Department should work with like-minded nations to build an International Cyber Crime Center that addresses the problem of sanctuary states—territories unwilling or unable to rein in cyber crime—and focuses on solving crimes and achieving successful prosecutions and to expand existing mechanisms.

- A cyber alliance should involve private companies, international law enforcement, and NGOs.

ADOPT A GREATER DEGREE OF TRANSPARENCY

Although public officials have warned about the threat of a "cyber Pearl Harbor" or "digital 9/11," the Task Force sees widespread cyber economic, political, and military espionage against defense, government, and private-sector networks as the most immediate threat to economic and national security interests. The capacity to launch a sudden strike that destroys or disrupts a large swath of critical infrastructure is most likely limited to a few nation-states. These actors should be deterred by the expectation that the United States could respond to a cyberattack through a combination of retaliatory cyber and kinetic attacks, as well as diplomatic and other measures.[46]

The U.S. government is more likely to be able to attribute a devastating attack to a specific state actor, especially if it comes during a geopolitical crisis, but the genesis of attacks at a lower threshold may remain unknown and will continue. These low-intensity attacks can have a long-term corrosive effect on the trust and integrity of the networks that are the foundation of the banking, transport, and communications systems. Furthermore, over time, the capability to conduct more damaging attacks will spread to states that may be harder to deter, as well as to extremists, lone wolves, criminal entities, and other nonstate actors.

It is widely assumed that offense has—and will continue to have in the foreseeable future—the advantage over defense in cyberspace. Improved defense and greater resiliency are necessary but not sufficient. The defense has to secure tens of millions of lines of code and billions of items of data across hundreds of networks and thousands of devices, which are often maintained by private actors and individuals. *As a result, offensive capabilities are required to deter attacks, and, if deterrence fails, to impose costs on the attackers.*

This offensive dominance, along with the problem of attribution and low barriers to entry, make cyberspace a highly unstable strategic environment. Given the speed of potential strikes, nation-states have strong incentive to strike first, to take out an adversary's communication, electric, and transportation grids before it strikes. Former secretary of defense Leon Panetta recently said that the United States may also consider preemptive strikes if it detects "an imminent threat of attack that will cause significant physical destruction in the United States or kill American citizens."[47] The concept of imminence in the cyber realm, however, remains legally and doctrinally nebulous.[48] This ambiguity makes coordination with allies more difficult since they may have a different legal interpretation of what is permissible. It increases the chances for miscalculation since legal boundaries can be useful for signaling and unclear ones can contribute to miscommunication, in addition to making it more difficult to predict international reactions to moves and countermoves in cyberspace.

After a long period in which U.S. officials hesitated to speak about offensive capabilities, over the last two years there have been a series of leaks to the press and public pronouncements on the development of cyber weapons. Reports in the *New York Times* and *Washington Post* have credited the United States and Israel with being behind Stuxnet, the malware designed to slow Iran's nuclear program as part of a secret operation code-named Olympic Games.[49]

Arguments in support of Stuxnet or other covert operations are based in part on the alternatives. That is, an attempt to slow Iran's nuclear program with malware that killed no one is politically and strategically preferable to commando raids, air strikes, or missile strikes that are likely to cause much greater physical damage and a number of deaths. Given the United States' high degree of vulnerability to cyberattacks, there is concern that an operation like Stuxnet may create blowback or provide cover for an adversary to conduct a similar attack. Iran appears to have accelerated its cyber programs after the attack. There is also a negative impact on the United States' ability to convince other states of the need for norms of peaceful conduct in cyberspace if they believe Washington has already used cyber weapons. But it is also true that many potential adversaries have been thinking about and developing offensive capabilities long before Stuxnet was ever developed, and the United States was no more vulnerable after Olympic Games was revealed than it was before. The public, however, is unable to fully participate in the debate on the merits of these types of uses of cyber weapons because of a high degree of secrecy. *The Task Force calls for a more open public discussion and, where appropriate, the declassification of information.*

Despite severe constraints in almost every other part of the defense budget, funding for computer network warfare is growing; the 2014 budget request includes $4.7 billion for cyberspace operations, a 20 percent increase from this year.[50] U.S. Cyber Command is reportedly expanding by more than fivefold, from nine hundred to forty-nine hundred personnel, and creating three types of forces: national mission forces, to protect critical infrastructure and defend against national-level threats; combat mission forces, assigned to the operational control of individual combatant commanders, to plan and execute attacks; and cyber protection forces, to defend the Defense Department's network.[51] Within the national mission forces, the Pentagon will reportedly create thirteen offensive teams by 2015 and twenty-seven within the combat mission forces to support the Pacific, Central, and other combatant commands as they plan offensive cyber operations.[52]

According to press reports, the Pentagon has developed classified rules of engagement for battle in cyberspace, which would guide commanders on when they could leave government networks to conduct offensive and defensive operations. In November 2012, President Obama reportedly signed Presidential Policy Directive 20, which "established principles and processes for the use of cyber operations," including the offensive use of computer attacks.[53] Offensive cyber operations outside a war zone are said to require presidential permission; even self-defense involving cyber operations outside military networks that could be construed as a use of force require presidential authorization. In addition, a legal review purportedly concluded that President Obama has the broad power to order a preemptive strike if the United States detects credible evidence of an imminent major cyberattack.[54]

This is progress compared with past reticence about offense, but U.S. government officials still publicly frame offensive military operations as defensive.[55] The Task Force supports the U.S. government's right to develop offensive capabilities, but calls for greater transparency about how and when such capabilities might be used. As the Defense Science Board argues, the United States needs to "clearly indicate that offensive cyber capabilities will be utilized (preemptively or in reaction, covertly or overtly), in combination with other instruments of national power, whenever the National Command Authority decides that it is appropriate."[56]

These statements should be linked to and reinforced by the United States' argument that the laws of war apply to cyberspace. State Department officials have said that that international humanitarian law can be extended to this new cyber domain, addressing the legal requirement of necessity in using force, what constitutes an act of force—"cyber activities that proximately result in death, injury, or significant destruction would likely be viewed as a use of force"—as well as the principles of proportionality, neutrality, and distinction.[57] But states like China question whether existing international laws apply to cyber and believe that cyberspace requires a new set of laws and treaties.

It is essential for the leading nations to agree on a set of norms for activity and engagement in cyberspace; a failure to agree will be destabilizing, increasing the chances of misperception, misunderstanding, and escalation. Perhaps even more disruptive to stability, nonstate actors frequently operate under the cover of a sovereign state. One country may see its action as permissible, the other as an act of war.

Determining the boundaries of cyber war is an area where the United States cannot go it alone. The State Department has been discussing these issues with the Groups of Governmental Experts (GGE) at the UN, which is made up of diplomats from fifteen countries, including Russia, China, Australia, Japan, and Egypt, and at the OSCE.[58] The State and Defense Departments should secure the cooperation of other states and civil society groups to clarify and expand the acceptance of these norms.

The *Tallinn Manual*, written by a group of international experts at the invitation of NATO's Cooperative Cyber Defence Centre of Excellence, addresses many of the specific applications of law to cyberspace.[59] The United States may not agree with all of the findings of the report, but this was a useful process that should be replicated in other forums with other groups of contributors. The State and Defense Departments, for example, should call together a group of legal advisers from Kenya, Brazil, China, India, Tunisia, South Africa, Turkey, and other important developing cyber powers to work on these questions.

Recent reporting suggests that China-based hackers broke into the computers of a company that monitors more than half of the oil and gas pipelines in North America. In this instance, it is uncertain whether the attackers were trying to steal industrial secrets to pass to Chinese companies or were planning to plant malware that would eventually shut down the energy system.[60] This ambiguity points to the need for continued discussions with partners and potential adversaries about the laws of armed conflict in cyberspace, the definition of legitimate targets, and how states signal intentions and control escalation. These discussions should focus on penetration and exploitation of industrial control systems, and are important in preventing miscalculations and misperception in cyberspace.

The State and Defense Departments should also continue to take active leadership in regional security groupings such as the OSCE, the ASEAN Regional Forum, and the Organization of American States on cyber-related confidence-building measures. These measures might include identifying points of contact within governments, joint training exercises, and developing crisis communication mechanisms.

SUMMARY OF RECOMMENDATIONS

- The Obama administration should clearly state that the United States has the right to conduct offensive operations.
- The State and Defense Departments should call together a group of legal advisers from important developing cyber powers to discuss applications of international law to cyberspace.

- The State and Defense Departments should take active leadership in regional security groupings such as the OSCE, the ASEAN Regional Forum, and the Organization of American States on cyber-related confidence-building measures.

DEVELOP A STRATEGY TO COUNTER CYBER ECONOMIC ESPIONAGE

U.S. government officials have clearly and accurately stated the threat of economic espionage to national and economic security. The Office of the National Counterintelligence Executive, for example, argues that "losses of sensitive economic information and technologies to foreign entities represent significant costs to U.S. national security."[61] Estimates of the effect of cyber espionage on U.S. GDP range from 0.1 percent ($25 billion) to 0.5 percent ($125 billion).

Having identified the threat, U.S. authorities must now act to combat it. Failing to address the espionage issue makes it far more likely that distrust and conflict will rule the future of cyberspace. Not only will nation-states seek to disrupt the capabilities of those they believe are stealing their trade secrets and intellectual property, but the number of actors could also multiply as companies and "privateers" use unregulated hackbacks and other illegal offensive cyber operations against hackers.

In February 2013, the Obama administration released the *Strategy on Mitigating the Theft of U.S. Trade Secrets.*[62] The strategy is primarily a continuation of policies already in place: promoting best practices to help industries protect against theft, enhancing U.S. law enforcement operations to increase investigations and prosecutions, and applying diplomatic pressure on foreign leaders to discourage theft. But the strategy does state that if diplomatic efforts are ineffective, the United States will use trade policy tools to press other governments for better protection and enforcement. These include mechanisms to target weaknesses in trade secret protection through enhanced use of the Special 301 process, the USTR's annual review of intellectual property protection and market access practices in foreign countries, and to include trade secret protections in new agreements like the Trans-Pacific Partnership.

Espionage, of course, has always been practiced. It is to be expected that nation-states will continue to conduct political and military cyber espionage, and international norms and agreements prohibiting general espionage are unlikely and undesirable. The State and Commerce

Departments, however, should work for a norm that bans large-scale commercial espionage, though this may be difficult to accomplish because some friends and allies of the United States do partake in the practice. In an effort to force these partners to justify their position, *the United States should explicitly open a dialogue on commercial espionage and state why the government and companies domiciled, owned, traded, or regulated within the United States do not legally steal corporate secrets and can and have been prosecuted for doing so.* President Obama, for example, has now publicly called out China on its cyber economic espionage campaign: "We've made it very clear to China and some other state actors that . . . we expect them to follow international norms and abide by international rules."[63]

The United States, the countries of the EU, Japan, and other like-minded countries should partake in a process similar to that used in building support for the proliferation security initiative (PSI), a global effort to prevent trafficking of weapons of mass destruction.[64] This would involve incorporating the prohibition against economic cyber espionage in multilateral and bilateral agreements, and perhaps eventually pursuing sanctions or other measures to restrict market access at the World Trade Organization (WTO). It would also require the prosecution of foreign nationals for economic espionage originating outside national boundaries. The Department of Justice recently set up a National Security Cyber Specialist program to help indict state-sponsored cyber attackers, although prosecution remains difficult.

In addition, the private sector should consider targeted civil lawsuits or international arbitration proceedings against enterprises that benefit from stolen data. Congress should amend the Computer Fraud and Abuse Act, strengthening the civil remedies provisions with specific dollar amounts in regard to the value of the theft and the civil penalties that can be leveraged against the attackers. The courts should also consider commercial damages. The precedent of this would be patent infringement cases, in which actual damages are generally tripled for those found guilty of willful infringement. If found guilty, a Chinese company would be raising costs for other companies, damaging its own credibility as a business partner, and driving a wedge between Chinese companies and state-backed hackers.

At home, the United States should implement an interagency economic counterespionage program that will help prevent foreign services and corporate competitors from stealing secrets from U.S. industry. The Obama administration appears to be moving in that direction, especially with the public naming of China as one of the major sources of cyber espionage by National Security Adviser Tom Donilon and a more forceful effort by senior diplomats to raise the issue with China. However, the issue extends far beyond China.

New policies should include directing national security resources to identify and collect intelligence on foreign efforts to target specific U.S. companies. An economic counterespionage policy of assisting specific U.S. companies when they have been individually targeted can avoid the conundrum of economic espionage, in which it is difficult to share the fruits of economic espionage fairly, equitably, and securely among U.S. industry. Foreign economic espionage usually benefits a state or a state-aligned corporation. The Treasury and Commerce Departments should develop sanctions against these offenders, and the United States should work through the WTO, INTERPOL, and other international organizations to develop norms and sanctions against economic espionage.

These policies would build on and take advantage of some of the existing programs for information sharing—the Defense Industrial Base cyber pilot (now known as the Enhanced Cybersecurity Services) and the Enduring Security Framework—but should also merge information collected by the intelligence agencies with the intelligence gathered by the private sector, as well as the firms conducting forensic investigations of the breaches. Merging the information collected by law enforcement and intelligence agencies with the type of information collected in a private-sector forensic investigation would result in a fundamentally different—and actionable—perspective on the threat.

SUMMARY OF RECOMMENDATIONS

- The United States should open a dialogue on commercial espionage and state why the government and companies domiciled, owned, traded, or regulated within the United States do not legally steal corporate secrets and can and have been prosecuted for doing so.
- The United States, the EU, Japan, and other like-minded partners should incorporate the prohibition against economic cyber espionage in multilateral and bilateral agreements, and perhaps eventually pursue sanctions or other measures to restrict market access at the World Trade Organization.

- The private sector should consider targeted civil lawsuits or international business arbitration proceedings against enterprises that benefit from stolen data.

- The United States should implement an interagency economic counterespionage program to prevent foreign services and corporate competitors from stealing secrets from U.S. industry. This would include directing national security resources to identify and collect intelligence on foreign efforts to target specific U.S. companies.

- This effort should merge information collected by the intelligence agencies with the intelligence gathered by the private sector, as well as by firms conducting forensic investigations of the breaches.

CLARIFY THE STATUTES SURROUNDING ACTIVE DEFENSE

As more cyberattacks on companies, the media, think tanks, civil society groups, and prominent individuals have become publicly known, the debate over whether private actors should be allowed to partake in active defense, or forms of defense that extend beyond a company's firewall, has become increasingly visible. The more offensive-oriented and legally questionable forms of these measures are sometimes referred to as "hacking back." In one survey, more than half of the respondents thought their companies should have the ability to hack back against their attackers. In another study, more than one-third admitted that they had already done so.[65]

The private sector and the U.S. government should work together to define and structure the concept of active cyber defense and to explore whether a regulated private security industry can successfully address the threats. Congress should consider amending statutes such as the Computer Fraud and Abuse Act so the private sector has certainty about what actions it can take to protect its property.

The promotion of active defense has been motivated by the rising capabilities of private actors and the recognition of the limitations on national authorities to respond effectively. Companies and others also recognize that firewalls, patching vulnerabilities, cyber hygiene, and other passive defenses are inadequate to defend against increasingly persistent, capable, and often state-backed adversaries. Proponents also argue that active defenses can raise the cost to attackers, in addition to gathering intelligence on them to prevent future attacks.

Active defense, however, is an ill-defined concept, and government and industry interpretations differ. It can include actions that are unlikely to be illegal, such as creating fake data and using honeypots or decoy networks to collect information on hackers, to the legally questionable, such as unilaterally taking down botnets and destroying the companies' own data held on third-party servers. Some have suggested the use of tracking beacons inside files that are at risk of being stolen, using disinformation, and planting fake data.

Active cyber defense presents significant threats and risks. A truly determined attacker may neither cease from current attacks nor be deterred from future attacks in the face of hacking back, but instead may escalate the conflict. Private actors could also damage innocent third parties, negatively affect diplomatic relations with states, or cause inadvertent escalation with a state actor. In addition, active defenses could interfere with an ongoing FBI investigation related to the same cyberattack that the active defense private actors are retaliating against.

SUMMARY OF RECOMMENDATIONS

- The private sector and the U.S. government should define and structure the concept of active cyber defense and explore whether a regulated private security industry can successfully address the threats.

- Congress should amend statutes such as the Computer Fraud and Abuse Act so the private sector has certainty about what actions it can take to protect its property.

CREATE A CYBER SERVICE

To prevent and respond to a catastrophic attack, the U.S. government will need to mobilize a well-trained cyber workforce. The current workforce is fragmented, divided among numerous agencies with different missions. No standard government process for recruitment, training, or evaluation exists. Talent shortages already exist and will worsen. More than 80 percent of the federal cybersecurity professional workforce is over forty years old, and only 5 percent is thirty years or younger. One-third of the federal workforce is expected to retire over the next three years.[66] One estimate puts future shortfalls at between twenty thousand and forty thousand people for many years out, and competition among government contractors, federal agencies, and the private sector for workers with hands-on experience defending networks from malicious attacks is intense.[67]

Over the long term, in order to expand the pipeline of people in cybersecurity, the United States will have to raise graduation rates in the fields of science, technology, engineering, and mathematics (STEM)—especially among women, who are particularly underrepresented in the field. In 2012, the Homeland Security Advisory Council offered recommendations on how DHS might improve recruitment, training, and retention by making the hiring process smoother, establishing two-year, community-college based training programs, enhancing opportunities for veterans, and establishing a pilot Cyber Reserve program that ensures DHS cyber alumni and other talented cybersecurity experts outside of government are known and available to DHS in times of need.[68] These DHS recommendations should be acted on.

Congress is also considering creating Cyber and Computer Network Incident Response Teams in the National Guard.[69] These teams, to be located in all fifty states and the District of Columbia, would leverage private-sector information technology (IT) expertise by combining both active and traditional Guard members. Governors would mobilize these teams for domestic incident response as well as to support existing DHS, DOJ, Secret Service, and state and local cyber efforts, and the secretary of defense would mobilize them for national defense under Title 10 status when necessary. Congress should move forward and create these National Guard teams.

These are worthwhile and useful recommendations that the Task Force supports, but workforce shortages are felt across almost every agency. *The government should develop a cyber service for use by multiple branches of the U.S. government.* There are risks that members of the service would not be familiar with the issues central to specific agencies, but these exist in other services as well and could be addressed through joint appointments, as happens now with FBI agents detailed to the CIA, for example. This is a more ambitious undertaking than improving cyber training for government employees within agencies. This would be a new professional career service comparable to the Foreign Service, National Clandestine Service, or the FBI's Special Agent program. Such an effort would create an entire culture and ethos of cyber operators, who could be detailed to different departments based on need.

SUMMARY OF RECOMMENDATIONS

- The United States should aim to raise graduation rates in the fields of science, technology, engineering, and mathematics to expand the pipeline of people in cybersecurity.
- The government should develop a cyber service for use by multiple branches of the U.S. government. This would be a new professional career service comparable to the Foreign Service, National Clandestine Service, or the FBI.

PASS CYBERSECURITY LEGISLATION

The public and private sector agree that defending critical infrastructure from cyberattacks will require robust information sharing and collaboration between government agencies and industry. Despite general bipartisan agreement on the serious nature of the cyber threat and the need for better information sharing, it is unclear whether the 113th Congress will be able to overcome politics and process to produce and pass a legislative package. The process of cyber legislation will be a test case of the 113th Congress's ability to manage the committee process through regular order. *The Task Force urges Congress to create and pass legislation that balances the need to meet the cyber threat with the protection of individual rights and private-sector liability.*

Public-private collaboration to combat cybersecurity threats has been enshrined as a policy priority at least since the Presidential Decision Directive 63, which former president Bill Clinton signed in 1998.[70] In response to PDD 63, the financial, electric, information technology, public transportation, nuclear, and other critical infrastructure sectors created Information Sharing and Analysis Centers (ISACs) to help disseminate threat information and provide incident response and risk mitigation. The National Infrastructure Protection Plan (NIPP), which was updated in 2009, calls for greater information sharing about cybersecurity threats.

Bank officials have said they sought support from the U.S. government during the large DDoS attacks in the fall of 2012 and spring of 2013. The NSA reportedly offered assistance in analyzing the attacks and evaluating remediation efforts, but bank officials have also criticized the quality and timeliness of shared information in the early stages of the attacks, as well as the larger difficulties of interfacing with the government.

Several legislative efforts have tried to give additional authorities to support information sharing, including the Cyber Intelligence Sharing and Protection Act (CISPA) in the House and the Cybersecurity Act of 2012 and the Strengthening and Enhancing Cybersecurity by Using Research, Education, Information, and Technology Act of 2012 (SECURE IT) in the Senate. CISPA passed in the House in 2012, but the Cybersecurity Act of 2012 did not receive enough votes to move to consideration in the Senate. Opposition revolved primarily around the nature of cyber standards for critical infrastructure companies, the protection of individual users' information, liability provisions for the private sector, and the role of the intelligence and defense communities in providing information to the private sector. CISPA was reintroduced in the 113th Congress and passed in the House in April 2013; President Obama has threatened to veto the bill if it is brought to and passes in the Senate. The Senate leadership has signaled the intention to bring additional cybersecurity legislation to the floor again, but the prospects for passage are uncertain.

The Task Force believes that President Obama's February 2013 executive order on cybersecurity was a positive move to improve the protection of critical infrastructure.[71] The order directs the Department of Homeland Security, Department of Justice, and Director of National Intelligence to share more information with privately owned critical national infrastructure such as the defense sector, utility networks, and the banking industry. The order also expands the Enhanced Cybersecurity Services (formerly known as the Defense Industrial Base pilot), a program that shares cybersecurity threat information with defense contractors and others with security clearances, to critical infrastructure companies. In an effort to raise security standards in the private sector through voluntary participation, the order calls for the establishment of a "cybersecurity framework." The framework is a voluntary set of cybersecurity best practices, developed by the National Institute of Standards and Technology (NIST) in conjunction with the private sector. DHS will work with the Department of Energy and other agencies, as well as industry councils, to implement the best practices laid out in the framework and identify incentives for companies to join the voluntary program.

Once NIST, with industry support, develops cybersecurity standards, it will be important for the White House to advocate for these standards in international bodies. The European Union is currently developing new standards on critical infrastructure, breach reporting, liability, and preparedness. Differing regulations will create difficulties for companies that have operations in both jurisdictions, and could pose problems as the two sides attempt to broker a free trade agreement.

The executive order, however, is limited in impact. It merely directs the government to do things that it was already authorized to do; the order does not address multidirectional information sharing and cannot grant companies liability protection if they are hit with a cyberattack because achieving these objectives would require legislation. Congressional efforts to improve information sharing are needed. Such efforts face obstacles related to committee jurisdictions, pressures from interest groups, and political considerations.

RECOMMENDATIONS

The Task Force calls on the U.S. Congress to create and pass legislation to meet the cyber threat soon. The legislation should have:

- a narrow focus on cybersecurity and cyber threats;
- mechanisms for the real-time sharing of information (including classified intelligence) between government and the private sector and among private-sector actors;
- a legal framework for the sharing of information;
- requirements to protect the identity of individual users and the protection of privacy in threat information shared with the government;
- protocols for sharing the information within the government;
- limited liability provisions for companies voluntarily involved in the information-sharing program; and
- a review process to prevent misuse of data by the U.S. government.

STRENGTHEN THE COORDINATING AUTHORITY OF THE NCCIC

Parallel to the legislative effort, the U.S. government should take organizational steps to improve information sharing and public-private cooperation. The Department of Homeland Security should bolster its capabilities in early warning cyber exercises and collaboration, as well as develop better mechanisms to draw upon the technical capabilities of other agencies.[72] The National Cybersecurity and Communications

Integration Center (NCCIC) should partake in joint threat and capabilities assessment with the private sector, and threat information should be shared earlier.

During the cyberattacks on banks, the U.S. government response was led by DHS's NCCIC, which is responsible for producing a common operating picture for cybersecurity across the federal government. Partners include the DOD, DOJ, FBI, and NSA, and its operational elements include the U.S. Computer Emergency Readiness Team (U.S.-CERT), Industrial Control Systems Cyber Emergency Response Team (ICS-CERT), and the National Coordinating Center for Telecommunications and Cyber Exercises. NCCIC also provides access for cleared individuals from the private sector to meet with a host of federal agencies. DHS organizes the Cyber Storm exercises. These drills, which include foreign governments, private-sector business, and individuals, are designed to improve interagency coordination, information sharing, and the collection and dissemination of response and recovery information.[73]

Many in the private sector and Congress are skeptical of DHS's emerging role as the primary civilian lead on several aspects of U.S. government cybersecurity. Some have questioned whether DHS has the administrative and technical capabilities to fulfill such a role. Critics question whether DHS has the strength to bring together all the agencies needed to coordinate information sharing and reach out to the private sector. Although NCCIC has recently gone through an internal reorganization, leadership turnover continues to be high, pointing to continued institutional turmoil. DHS and NCCIC will have to take steps to reassure the public and private sectors that they are capable of taking the lead on many cyber issues.

SUMMARY OF RECOMMENDATIONS

- The Department of Homeland Security (DHS) should bolster its capabilities in early warning cyber exercises and collaboration and develop better mechanisms to draw upon the technical capabilities of other agencies.

- The National Cybersecurity and Communications Integration Center (NCCIC) should partake in joint threat and capabilities assessment with the private sector, and threat information should be shared earlier.

INCREASE CYBER POLICYMAKERS' AUTHORITY

Coordination problems continue to bedevil the interagency process. Organizational change is important for supporting all three pillars of digital policy: alliances, trade, and governance. Within the State Department, Internet issues are divided among the Office of the Cyber Coordinator, Bureau of Economic and Business Affairs, and Bureau of Democracy, Human Rights, and Labor. Across the entire U.S. government at least fourteen government bureaus, divisions, and departments collaborate with international agencies and organizations on cyberspace issues. This not only leads to coordination and messaging problems but makes it difficult for those outside of the United States without great knowledge of the workings of cyber policy to know with whom to interact.

At present, without clear legal authority, the NCCIC must make multiple requests from other agencies for information that could help defend the private sector. Its authority should be increased and clarified. *The position of director of the NCCIC should be elevated to an undersecretary or even a deputy secretary rank, Senate-confirmed position—as is the director of the National Counterterrorism Center.* This would not fully resolve issues of interagency coordination, but it would give the holder of the position increased authority to coordinate and make requests of other agencies.

Over the next two years, the State Department should review the Office of the Cyber Coordinator and consider replacing the post with an assistant secretary in charge of a cyber bureau. If the position remains, the Office of the Coordinator for Cyber Issues should lead the U.S. international position on the Internet across organizations where Internet governance discussions are conducted.

In addition, following the model of the German foreign ministry and UK Foreign and Commonwealth Office, *the State Department should post cyber attachés—Foreign Service officers specializing in cyber issues—in important capitals* such as London, Beijing, Brussels, Brasilia, Ankara, Nairobi, and Delhi.

In the White House, the special assistant to the president and cybersecurity coordinator is currently on the national security staff. *Over the next two years, the White House should review whether the cybersecurity coordinator should also be part of the National Economic Council and the Office of Science and Technology Policy.* The wearing of three hats may give the coordinator the necessary authority and influence to shape a more cohesive strategy.

SUMMARY OF RECOMMENDATIONS

- The position of director of the NCCIC should be elevated to an undersecretary or even a deputy secretary rank, Senate-confirmed position—like the director of the National Counterterrorism Center.

- The State Department should review the Office of the Cyber Coordinator and consider replacing the post with an assistant secretary in charge of a cyber bureau.

- The State Department should post cyber attachés—Foreign Service officers specializing in cyber issues—at important diplomatic outposts.

- The White House should review whether the cybersecurity coordinator, currently on the national security staff, should also be part of the National Economic Council and the Office of Science and Technology Policy.

TRADE, INNOVATION, AND GROWTH

The Task Force believes all future trade agreements should contain a goal of fostering the free flow of information and data across national borders while protecting intellectual property and developing an interoperable global regulatory framework for respecting the privacy rights of individuals.

The General Agreement on Trade in Services of the World Trade Organization came into force in 1995 and expanded trade rules from goods to services, including financial, telecommunications, and cloud and other Internet-based services. The formalization of these Internet principles in new trade agreements would be an important step.

The U.S.-Korea Free Trade Agreement calls on the two countries to "refrain from imposing or maintaining unnecessary barriers to electronic information flows across borders." The Trans-Pacific Partnership (TPP), the upcoming U.S.-European trade negotiations, and future bilateral agreements should all guarantee the free flow of information across borders and proper steps to protect copyright holders and intermediaries, and that servers need not be located in countries where companies provide services and products.

Because most of the discussion on the TPP occurs behind closed doors, it is difficult to gauge progress on it. Vietnam, one of the potential signatories, is perhaps a more extreme example of the potential complications of getting states with different political systems and levels of development to refrain from imposing barriers on the free flow of information as part of a trade agreement. In January 2012, the Vietnamese government convicted and sentenced five activists for blogging in support of freedom of expression.

RECOMMENDATIONS

Several previous governmental and private efforts have done important work in developing the basic principles of digital trade and information flows.[74] *Drawing on these previous reports and policy papers, the Task Force recommends the following:*

- Governments should not require that facilities, servers, or information be located in specific countries or regions.
- Regulators should not discriminate between domestic and foreign producers.
- Governments should provide appropriate limitations of liabilities for Internet intermediaries.
- Trade policy should support a trusted environment where personal data, intellectual property, privacy, and cybersecurity are all protected.
- Bilateral and multilateral trade agreements should guarantee the free flow of information and data across national borders.
- Regulations affecting data transfer should be transparent, provided for by law, and consistent with the maximal protection of privacy, user security, and free expression.
- Governments should promote investment in expansion of Internet networks and high-speed broadband.
- Governments should maximize the availability and use of the spectrum in a transparent and nondiscriminatory manner.
- Public policy should be technology neutral and foster a diversity of platforms.

To build on these recommendations and further promote U.S. digital trade, the Task Force also recommends the following:

- The Trans-Pacific Partnership, the upcoming U.S.-European trade negotiations, and future bilateral agreements should guarantee the free flow of information across borders.

- The United States, along with its trading partners, should create a digital due process so that requests for content removal and user data are consistent with international practices.

- The United States and others should make transfer of data between governments more transparent and efficient by improving the Mutual Legal Assistance Treaty system.

- With its Japanese and European counterparts, the USTR should coordinate pressure on India and Brazil on procurement regulations, location requirements, and other nontariff barriers to trade.

- The United States should protect intellectual property, while preserving the rights of users to access lawful content.

- The United States should help create an environment in which the Internet economy flourishes.

CREATE A DIGITAL DUE PROCESS

International trade agreements are important, as they will help define norms and set standards that can be extended to other parts of the world. While the Trans-Pacific Partnership proceeds, signs of activity now surround the Transatlantic Trade and Investment Partnership (TTIP) after almost fifteen years of unproductive discussions. A high-level working group has given the go-ahead for the two sides to begin negotiations, and the United States and EU are expected to look for opportunities to reduce, eliminate, or prevent barriers to trade in services and enhance the compatibility of regulations and standards. TTIP is expected to include provisions that facilitate the movement of cross-border data flows. *The Task Force welcomes movement on the TTIP, but cautions that a number of important transatlantic differences need to be resolved.*

There are significant challenges in the transatlantic relationship outside of the scope of the TTIP. The EU is currently revising the 1995 Data Protection Directive, which regulates the processing of personal data within the European Union, and many of the proposed changes appear prohibitively expensive and prescriptive. The European Commission has estimated that the revisions could save businesses throughout Europe 2.3 billion euros by harmonizing and simplifying standards. However, the UK Ministry of Justice has countered with an estimate that the cost to the United Kingdom alone would be between 100 million and 360 million pounds a year.[75] The UK government has also opposed the one-size-fits-all approach found in the directive, noting that all data collectors—from small businesses to multinationals—will have to follow the regulations for completing data protection, impact assessments, and the hiring of data protection officers.

Some of the proposed revisions appear unworkable. The European Parliament is considering proposals that would create data portability—individual users would be able to transfer personal posts, photos, and videos from one online service site to another "without hindrance"—and the "right to be forgotten." Users would also be able to obtain details about what data companies hold on them. Those firms that fail to follow the data portability regulation could face penalties of up to 2 percent of global revenue. U.S. critics have argued that the provision is overly broad, corrosive to innovation, and could disrupt businesses' access to data. Though data portability might increase security by allowing users to switch to more secure providers instead of staying locked into less secure servers, by concentrating a lifetime of a user's data in one place, it could also increase vulnerability. With a "right to be forgotten," users can demand that publicly available information or replications on websites and search engines be deleted. Failing to delete the information could lead to fines of up to 1 percent of a company's revenue. The European Network and Information Security Agency, however, found that "a purely technical and comprehensive solution to enforce the right in the open Internet is generally impossible."[76]

European policymakers have raised concerns about the U.S. government accessing the data of European citizens stored on the servers of American companies through powers granted by the Patriot Act and the Foreign Intelligence Surveillance Amendments Act. These processes are not exclusive to the United States; several countries, including a number of member countries of the EU, have wide-ranging provisions that allow access to cloud-stored data outside their respective jurisdictions.

As a result, policymakers and business leaders need to foster a digital due process so that requests for content removal and user data are consistent with international practices. Countries should develop a robust approach to digital due process that facilitates proper legal process for resolving domestic and foreign requests for information. This is an area where the United States can exert a great deal of influence as a positive model and where American technology companies are taking the lead. Google, Twitter, LinkedIn, Microsoft, and other companies now issue transparency reports that detail the number of requests they receive from government law enforcement for data on users around the world.

SUMMARY OF RECOMMENDATIONS

- Policymakers and business leaders from social media, data processing, cloud computing, and other data-intensive industries need to foster a digital due process so that requests for content removal and user data are consistent with international practices.

- The United States and EU should develop a robust approach to digital due process that facilitates proper legal processes for resolving domestic and foreign requests for information.

IMPROVE THE EFFICIENCY OF THE MLATS

Government authorities need to work across borders to fight crime and prevent terrorist attacks, but many lawful intercept regulations—demands for communications network data for the purpose of analysis or evidence—are inconsistent and often burdensome to business and overly broad, threatening user privacy.

The transfer of data between governments can be made more transparent and efficient through improving the Mutual Legal Assistance Treaty (MLAT) system, through which nations agree to share information and evidence during criminal proceedings.

RECOMMENDATIONS

- MLATs should explicitly define the modes of communication they cover, require governments and companies to provide explicit protections of individual rights and personal data, and include explicit timetables for cooperation and response by governments.

- When the laws of more than one state apply to data, the higher of the standards should be applied, and MLATs should require governments to regularly disclose when and why personal data is requested.

PRESSURE CHINA, INDIA, AND BRAZIL

U.S.-EU efforts to reach agreements on how data is collected, managed, and shared, as well as other trade and investment regulations, are important because they help set a template for rising economies such as China, India, and Brazil. *The United States and its partners should maintain steady pressure on these three countries to uphold international standards.*

Beijing's efforts to restrict the flow of information and to encourage "indigenous innovation" through government procurement, technology transfer, and location requirements have attracted the lion's share of negative attention. But India has also requested access to proprietary source code, pursued initiatives that will allow broad compulsory licensing of critical technologies, and recently proposed regulations that would force technology companies to manufacture locally if they want to sell to the government. The motivation for these demands is often opaque; policies can be driven by real security concerns, the desire to promote competing technology standards and strengthen domestic firms, or some combination thereof.

The United States has had some limited success with China through the Joint Commission on Commerce and Trade and at high-level summits such as the Strategic and Economic Dialogue; Beijing has promised not to discriminate against foreign technology or mandate domestic encryption and wireless authentication technologies, and to strengthen intellectual property rights provisions.

RECOMMENDATIONS

- The United States, in coordination with Japan and the EU, should maintain pressure on China and should exert similar pressure on India and Brazil.
- If the pressure is ineffective and these countries continue to discriminate against foreign goods and services, the United States should consider, depending on the political and economic context, a range of possible responses, including, but not limited to, threatening to

withdraw or limit unilateral benefits granted to India and Brazil and suspending or withdrawing duty-free treatment of Indian and Brazilian goods subject to the Generalized System of Preferences (GSP) to ensure those countries "provide equitable and reasonable access to [their] markets," one of the GSP's fundamental criteria.

- The United States should refine the content of and globalize Asia-Pacific Economic Cooperation innovation policy principles, entitled Promoting Effective, Non-Discriminatory, and Market-Driven Innovation Policy, so that they apply outside of the APEC region.

PROTECT INTELLECTUAL PROPERTY WHILE PRESERVING THE RIGHTS OF USERS

Protecting intellectual property is a cornerstone of U.S. innovation and competitiveness. *The United States should continue to work to remove and limit the availability of pirated content and counterfeit products online.*

Blocking or censoring sites and files has some short-lived effects, but does not appear to decrease the long-term availability of pirated content on the Internet. Pirates often respond to the takedown of file sharing sites by spreading the stolen content over hundreds of services. "Warning models," such as notice and takedown, or "graduated responses"— users are warned that illegal material has been downloaded to their account and the Internet service provider may slow down Internet speeds, or cut users off entirely, after a certain number of violations— have worked in some countries but not in others.

The real culprits are dishonest advertising services and malware distributors that use pirated content to attract users. Cutting off the advertisement flow and shutting down the malware companies would address the majority of this problem. In addition, some of the technical and political means used in blocking websites threaten innovation and the free flow of information.

RECOMMENDATIONS

- The United States should work with advertising agencies and trade groups to cut off the flow of advertising and payments to sites hosting illegal materials.
- The mechanisms for requesting sanctions should be public and transparent.

- The Department of Commerce and the USTR should continue to pressure other nations to curtail the activities of pirate hosting sites and consider trade sanctions when they do not.

HELP THE INTERNET ECONOMY FLOURISH

The United States should continue to work with its trading partners from a position of strength at home. More broadly, policymakers need to help create an environment in which the Internet economy flourishes.

Given the rapidly changing nature of information technology and the complexity of networked industries, policymakers should strive for a relatively hands-off regulatory approach. Regulation should be reserved for those situations where it is necessary to intervene to ensure fair, transparent, and nondiscriminatory market behavior. Furthermore, regulations should also be technology neutral and promote competition so as to preserve cyberspace's openness to new devices, applications, and services.

The United States should develop a strong workforce able to pursue new market opportunities and create the next wave of innovation. Despite a large pool of unemployed workers, employers currently struggle to find skilled talent to fill job openings. In a 2012 survey conducted by the American Society for Training & Development, 84 percent of respondents reported a skills gap in their organizations.[77] Employers in the STEM fields are suffering in particular. Jobs related to cloud computing, for example, are expected to grow annually by 26 percent through 2015. Some 1.7 million cloud-related jobs, however, were not filled in 2012 because job seekers did not have the proper training and qualifications.[78] As previously noted, the United States will need to raise graduation rates in STEM fields.

The Obama administration and U.S. Congress should also address the needs of today's workforce by simplifying the processes for accessing public-sector training dollars, improving the performance of community colleges, and making community colleges more responsive to local workforce requirements.

Furthermore, the United States should pass meaningful immigration reform to attract and retain highly skilled talent. The influx of new people has been critical to maintaining the competitiveness and creativity of the American economy. According to a 2007 study by Duke University and the University of California, Berkeley, one-fourth of the technology companies started in the United States from 1995 to 2005 had at least one foreign-born founder; a 2012 Kauffman Foundation report found that almost one-third of firms in the semiconductor sector, 28 percent in computer fields, and 25 percent in innovation and manufacturing-related services had one immigrant founder.[79] Openness is essential, and the United States needs to remain the place where the most talented and skilled still yearn to come.

SUMMARY OF RECOMMENDATIONS

- Policymakers should strive for a relatively hands-off regulatory approach. Regulation should be reserved for those situations where it is necessary to intervene to ensure fair, transparent, and nondiscriminatory market behavior.
- Regulations should be technology neutral, promote competition among different providers, and preserve cyberspace's openness to new devices, applications, and services.
- The United States needs to develop a strong workforce able to pursue new market opportunities and create the next wave of innovation. In particular, the United States needs to raise graduation rates in STEM fields.
- The United States should simplify the process for accessing public sector training dollars and improve the performance of community colleges to make them more responsive to local workforce requirements.
- The United States should pass comprehensive immigration reform to attract and retain highly skilled talent.

INTERNET GOVERNANCE AND THE FREE FLOW OF INFORMATION AND KNOWLEDGE

The free and open Internet of today developed under an informal, decentralized process that involved all parties with a stake in its governance. The United States played a dominant role in shaping it. But now, as the Internet reaches adulthood, change is happening. *The United States has a choice: pursue an ultimately fruitless course to maintain its perceived dominance to date, or adjust to changing realities and the emergence of new Internet powers in the developing world. The Task Force urges the U.S. government to face the new reality.*

As noted earlier, the United States and other countries stood on their principles to exclude the Internet from a telecommunications treaty at the December 2012 meeting of the World Conference on International Telecommunications in Dubai.

The United States has legitimate concerns about certain outcomes in the ITU; it wants interconnectivity issues, such as packet switching, to stay in the hands of technical and private actors, rather than placed under the control of governments. *But the United States needs to address the legitimate access, infrastructure, and security concerns of developing countries.* Leadership is required, and Washington cannot continue to beat back efforts for reform without an alternative. Developing countries need to recognize the benefits of the bottom-up, nongovernmental approach.

RECOMMENDATIONS

The Task Force believes the United States should articulate and advocate a vision of Internet governance that includes emerging Internet powers and expands and strengthens the multi-stakeholder process.

As part of the effort to help ensure cyberspace remains an open and global platform for sharing information and knowledge, the Task Force recommends the following:

- The United States should work with the ITU more consistently and persistently.

- The Commerce and State Departments should provide greater support to the Government Advisory Committee of ICANN and the Internet Governance Forum.

- The United States should explore alternative venues for discussing the challenges of Internet governance and cybersecurity.

- The United States should invest in education, training, and equipment upgrades in potential partners in the developing world, with the Departments of Justice and State setting aside budget allocations for this purpose.

- Partnering with other governments and NGOs like the Global Network Initiative, Washington should help demonstrate concrete social, political, and economic payoffs from an open Internet.

- Working with civil society groups, the United States should develop guidelines on the exports of surveillance and other dual-use technologies.

PROMOTING AN INCLUSIVE AGENDA

The United States needs to promote an inclusive agenda with three parts:

First, the United States should work with the ITU more consistently and persistently. One of the lessons of the WCIT is that the United States needs to engage early and often. Ambassador Terry Kramer was appointed head of the U.S. delegation to WCIT only in August 2012. Six months is not adequate preparation time for mobilizing government and private-sector resources, especially when China was organizing for close to three years. The United States needs a tenacious international presence led by the White House to combat the ITU's incrementalism and it should appoint delegations for international forums early on. The United States should also work with like-minded nations to identify and build international support for a candidate for the ITU secretary-general position who is committed to the multistakeholder process.

Second, the State and Commerce Departments should make the multistakeholder model more inclusive and robust. The Government Advisory Committee of ICANN, which provides advice on public policy issues and the governance of ICANN as a whole, should receive the support it needs to become more efficient and transparent so that it can be seen as an effective place for governments to advise and shape policy and be accountable to the public at large. The Internet Governance Forum (IGF), an open forum established by the World Summit on the Information Society in 2006 and convened by the UN secretary-general, should be given more attention and sufficient financial support.[80] The annual one-week meetings are not enough, and the system of regional IGFs should be strengthened with financial support to the IGF Secretariat and for developing world participants to attend.

Third, the United States should explore alternative venues for discussing the challenges of Internet governance and cybersecurity. Working with 193 countries at the beginning, however, is too unwieldy. Instead, the agenda should be crafted through smaller ad hoc groups or regional groupings. The Major Economies Forum on Energy and Climate, for example, includes dialogue among developed and developing economies as well as concrete initiatives and joint ventures to increase the supply of clean energy, and the Global Counterterrorism Forum includes twenty-nine countries plus the EU to share expertise and identify needs. Membership of ad hoc cyber groups would change depending on topic and expertise and would address discrete problems. The United States should work with some critical countries, including but not limited to China, Brazil, India, Russia, Turkey, Tunisia, Kenya, the United Kingdom, Estonia, Sweden, Hungary, and South Korea.

A useful forum is the Open Government Partnership, cofounded by the United States and Brazil.[81] More than forty-five signatories from the developed and developing world have committed themselves to greater transparency, civic participation, and accountability. This is an ideal group to develop complementary principles for cyberspace, and a working group—not chaired by the United States—should start defining how they would apply to Internet governance.

More narrowly, the Departments of State and Commerce should encourage a forum at which developing countries and users can address cybersecurity and other technical concerns without having to turn to the ITU. The National Telecommunications and Information Administration, for example, held a meeting in March 2013 in London to follow up on the issue of spam and unsolicited email. These discussions should be coordinated with and feed back into the cybersecurity work of ICANN and IGF.

It is not enough just to build alternative processes and institutions; the United States also needs to give developing countries the capacity to effectively use international processes and institutions. The United States should invest in education, training, and equipment upgrades in potential partners in the developing world, with the Departments of Justice and State needing to set aside budget allocations for this purpose. The Department of Justice has conducted international training, and over the last three years, the Office of the Coordinator for Cyber Issues in the Department of State partnered with Kenya, Senegal, and Ghana to cohost cybersecurity and cyber crime workshops. Meeting the scale of demand and reaching beyond Africa, however, will take an expansion of resources and full-time staff in the Office of the Coordinator for Cyber Issues.

Private industry should also be encouraged to invest in cybersecurity in the emerging economies. For instance, the Korea Information Security Agency is working with Korea Telecom to help build Rwanda's Computer Emergency Response Team. In March 2013, the U.S. Agency for International Development announced a project with Cisco to set up two networking academies to provide ICT skills training in Burma.

SUMMARY OF RECOMMENDATIONS

- The United States should explore alternative venues for discussing the challenges of Internet governance and cybersecurity.

- The Departments of State and Commerce should encourage a forum at which developing countries and users can address cybersecurity and other technical concerns without having to turn to the ITU.

- The United States needs to give developing countries the capacity to use international processes and institutions effectively.

- Private industry should be encouraged to invest in cybersecurity in the emerging economies.

DEMONSTRATE THE BENEFITS OF AN OPEN INTERNET

The United States has been clear about the political context of Internet freedom. Numerous U.S. officials have rightfully stressed that human rights and freedoms apply in cyberspace. In July 2012, the United States cosponsored a Swedish-led resolution in the UN Human Rights Council to protect the free speech of individuals online.[82] The resolution, which was approved by all forty-seven members of the council, including China and Cuba, recognizes "the global and open nature of the Internet as a driving force in accelerating progress towards development in its various forms." *The new approach to Internet governance needs to include a comprehensive vision of the benefits of the free flow of information and knowledge.*

The State Department's spending on Internet freedom initiatives from 2008 to 2012 totaled approximately $100 million and includes funding for the development of anticensorship and secure communications technology, as well as digital safety training for activists and emergency response support for civil society organizations under threat.

Washington can also help demonstrate other concrete social and political payoffs from an open Internet. The United Nations, or a regional security organization such as the OSCE or the ASEAN Regional Forum, should develop secure arenas for the uploading of verifiable videos during civil or international conflict. This is part of a more positive vision of how keeping the Internet open can help advance accountability and justice.

The most powerful argument for Internet openness is economic. U.S. officials have consistently noted that filtering and blocking content can have deleterious effects on investment and innovation as well as on freedom and self-expression. As former secretary of state Hillary Clinton said in reference to China and others, "In the short term, even perhaps in the medium term, those governments may succeed in maintaining a segmented Internet. But those restrictions will have long-term costs that threaten one day to become a noose that restrains growth and development."[83] Yet numerous governments continue to believe that they can reap economic benefits while maintaining tight control, and they may look to the Chinese example to bolster their argument. As noted earlier, though a growing body of data link economic growth in developed economies to the Internet, the research is lacking for developing economies. The United States should press the OECD and other international agencies to broaden and deepen actionable research.

These arguments will empower civil groups and private actors within other countries to push for a more open Internet. Such arguments may be more effective if they are segregated from specific American foreign policy goals. That is, although the free flow of information should remain high on the official U.S. diplomatic agenda, it is better if the notion is pushed by local companies and nongovernmental organizations so as not to allow authoritarian regimes to paint the free flow of information as an American idea or as another example of outside interference in sovereign matters.

An organization like the Global Network Initiative (GNI) is an important partner in the effort. GNI is a collection of companies, investors, NGOs, and academics advocating for users' rights to freedom of expression and privacy.[84] Currently, eleven companies have signed on with the GNI, and two are observers. Although GNI has recently entered into a two-year collaboration with eight Europe-based telecommunications companies, its efforts would be strengthened by greater participation of foreign information technology firms, especially from the developing world.

SUMMARY OF RECOMMENDATIONS

- The United States needs to actively "sell" all the benefits of the free flow of information and knowledge, including economic and social advantages.

- Washington should promote the right to access through the Open Government Partnership. A working group, not chaired by the United States, should define how to apply the Open Government Partnership's principles of transparency, participation, and accountability to Internet access.

- The United Nations, or a regional security organization such as the OSCE or the ASEAN Regional Forum, should develop secure arenas for the uploading of verifiable videos during civil or international conflict.

- The United States should continue to make the case that filtering or blocking content will have negative effects on investment and innovation. The United States should encourage the OECD and other international agencies to conduct research that links economic growth in developing economies to the Internet.

- The United States should continue to press for the free flow of information online, but in many instances it should step back and let local companies and nongovernmental organizations lead the public argument.

DEVELOP GUIDELINES ON THE EXPORTS OF DUAL-USE TECHNOLOGIES

The difficulty with Internet technologies is that they are inherently dual use. Governments and private actors can use them for legitimate purposes, including network and computer security investigations, research, and protection. When used legitimately and legally for national security and law enforcement, they can enhance the security and safety of the individual user. On the other hand, authoritarian states are relying on these technologies to track opposition and facilitate human rights abuses. *The United States and its partners need to carefully address the dangers of exporting dual-use technologies while not overly regulating exports. Partnerships with civil society, NGOs, and the private sector are the best route to effective guidelines.*

Invasive technologies with the capability to track the movement of their citizens, read emails and mobile texts, listen in on phone calls, and scan online photos are in increasing demand by governments. Software developed by the UK-based Gamma Group was used to monitor human rights activists in Bahrain and Egypt. Narus, a subsidiary of Boeing, sold surveillance equipment to Egypt, and Internet surveillance and censorship technology from California-based Blue Coat Systems was found being used in Syria and China.[85]

Governments in Europe are already moving to control the exports of such equipment. In March 2012, the Council of Europe banned EU companies from selling monitoring equipment to Iran. In September, the British government imposed export controls on Gamma Group's FinSpy surveillance tool, and the government is reportedly considering international and/or EU-level agreements on the export of surveillance equipment. Sometime in 2013, the European Commission will introduce rules to improve the monitoring of EU exports of technology that can be used to censor or block websites and monitor mobile communications. The European Commission will regularly update a list of restricted products and countries.

The Task Force warns that the legislative approach is heavy-handed and inflexible and could generate unintended outcomes. Technology sanctions on Iran and Syria, for example, have made it difficult for dissident groups to access technologies that can evade electronic surveillance and censorship. In addition, the intense globalization of sophisticated development, production, and distribution of information and communication technology products renders many controls ineffective and can pose significant competitive disadvantages where one country imposes controls and another does not. For example, until the mid-1990s, encryption products and technologies were subject to unilateral U.S. munitions export controls, creating a major disincentive to develop products with security features employing U.S. technology. This put the United States at a huge competitive disadvantage with other countries at a time when strong encryption capabilities and products were already widely available internationally. Transferring encryption export controls from the U.S. Munitions List to the Commerce Control List in 1996 broke this cycle, and U.S. companies were able to become highly innovative and globally competitive in the development of commercial products with encryption features.

Unreasonable or excessive controls, whether applied to encryption or other technologies, entail much industry effort and restraint without resulting in purposeful or effective control. This fact is highly relevant to commercial ICT products and technology, where the utility of controls is undermined by commoditization, high volume distribution, global and decentralized development and production capabilities, ubiquitous networks and computing capability, and the offsetting benefits of globalizing the ICT revolution.

In addressing national security, foreign policy, or other government concerns, policymakers should avoid imposing export or other trade controls on generally available ICT products and technologies, except under narrow and justifiable circumstances. Rather, government policies should accommodate and encourage more effective and creative ways to address overall national security and other policy challenges, opportunities, and options.

A good example is the aforementioned Global Network Initiative, which requires companies to conduct human rights assessments before introducing products into new markets. Public attention to sales of these technologies from the media, as well as congressional hearings and testimony, may convince others of the utility of adopting similar policies.

SUMMARY OF RECOMMENDATIONS

- The United States should avoid a heavy-handed and inflexible legislative approach to export controls. Unreasonable or excessive controls entail much industry effort and restraint without resulting in purposeful or effective control.

- Policymakers should avoid imposing export or other trade controls on generally available ICT products and technologies, except under narrow and justifiable circumstances.

- Government policies should accommodate and encourage more effective and creative ways to address overall national security and other policy challenges, opportunities, and options, such as the Global Network Initiative.

Conclusion: An Open, Global, Secure, and Resilient Internet Is in Everyone's Interest

The Internet is now an essential tool for governments, companies, and individuals. No one can be certain of the future economic, social, political, and cultural opportunities that will emerge; the technology is still evolving, and billions of people have yet to go online and communicate, create, and build. What is certain is that cyberspace's importance will only increase. The United States is well positioned to reap the benefits, known and unknown, of the expansion and deepening of this world-wide platform for sharing information and data.

Yet the next two billion users will come from the developing economies, and there needs to be greater institutional flexibility to respond to these new users' needs and demands. There are threats that travel through the Internet and threats to the Internet. Cyberspace is now an arena for strategic competition among states, and a growing number of actors—state and nonstate—use the Internet for conflict, espionage, and crime. Societies are becoming more vulnerable to widespread disruption as energy, transportation, communication, and other critical infrastructure are connected through computer networks.

At the same time, the open, global Internet is at risk. Nations are reasserting sovereignty and territorializing cyberspace. The justifications are many—national security, economic interest, cultural sensitivity—but the outcome of blocking, filtering, and regulating is the same: a fragmented Internet and a decline in global free expression. Diplomacy has done little to close the gap between those who support the private-sector-led, multi-stakeholder model of Internet governance and those who want a stronger role for the state in cyberspace governance under the auspices of the United Nations and the ITU.

The United States should be realistic about what can be accomplished. Digital policy always involves real trade-offs between privacy, security, openness, innovation, and the protection of intellectual property. Multiple sources of power and influence, divergent values, and clashing interests all complicate policymaking within countries and across borders. A grand bargain that covers all the concerns of content producers and technology innovators is equally unlikely as one between liberal democracies and authoritarian states.

In this context, the Task Force sees its role as not only suggesting policies that will help keep the Internet open, global, secure, and resilient, but also as framing the problem so policymakers, business leaders, and individual users better understand what is at stake and are aware of the trade-offs and consequences, expected and unintended, of what those policy decisions may be. To that end, the Task Force recommends that the Council on Foreign Relations and its members continue to bring the public and private sectors, technologists, and policymakers together to debate these issues, both at home and abroad.

U.S. policymakers need to be proactive. The trends do not look good, but by building a cyber alliance, making the free flow of information a part of all future trade agreements, and articulating an inclusive and robust vision of Internet governance, Washington can limit the effects of a fragmenting Internet. The United States can no longer rely on its role as the progenitor of the Internet to claim the mantle of leadership. Rather, it can exert a positive influence on cyberspace by working to convince the next wave of users that an open and global Internet is in all of our interests.

Additional Views

The work of the Independent Task Force and its report, *Defending an Open, Global, Secure, and Resilient Internet*, provides a valuable starting point for a substantive public discussion about U.S. digital policy. The report defines many of the challenges facing U.S. policymakers and provides concrete recommendations for the U.S. government and major stakeholders.

Most important, the report provides a framework for more fundamental questions to be asked about the formulation of U.S. digital policy.

Current U.S. policy supports existing institutions in the multi-stakeholder governance system in order to promote an open Internet. First and foremost, policy leaders must ask: To what degree is this strategy in the nation's interest? Supporters of the "bottom-up" concept of governance argue that an open Internet promotes innovation. But how does this system resolve the inherent tensions between nurturing innovation, protecting the outcomes of innovation, and preserving legacy innovation? Similarly, does this system offer protections for innovators and consumers alike? Does it provide for adequate enforcement, accountability, and, ultimately, the predictable, transparent, and sustained rule of law?

The report also paves the way for policy leaders to define the meaning of an open Internet. What is the appropriate balance between openness and enforcement? What defines the limits of information sharing between governments and the private sector? How is information sharing reconciled with the privacy rights and related concerns of citizens and consumers?

In the context of global commerce, the United States considers the World Trade Organization, which is rooted in the rule of law, to be the guarantor of an open and free trade system. Does the United States similarly seek an open and free Internet with consensus rules to protect human rights, free speech, and intellectual property? If so, which institutions will most effectively guarantee enforcement of core national values in the Internet environment?

There are no easy answers to these questions, as the Task Force found. The U.S. government can help by setting appropriate domestic expectations about the opportunities and limits of the Internet. But difficult questions are too often punted when domestic political consensus proves elusive. Nevertheless, consensus is necessary before the United States can pursue and secure appropriate global cyber policy objectives.

U.S. policy leaders cannot afford to abdicate their role in developing a comprehensive national digital policy. The Task Force's report should serve as a springboard for challenging existing policy assumptions and working toward a digital policy that serves U.S. economic and national security interests.

Naotaka Matsukata

I strongly support the thrust and virtually all of the recommendations of this thoughtful and far-ranging report, particularly the need for the United States to provide leadership in building new alliances and articulating international norms to sustain the viability of this vital capacity in the face of the challenges the report identifies.

My small reservations concern statements about the organization of the U.S. government. The report observes, implicitly critically, that "no single individual or agency is in charge, short of the president." In my view, that is as it should be. The issues surrounding the Internet, as the report makes so amply clear, touch on virtually every aspect of government policy, domestic and international. It would be beyond the span of any individual to try to manage that diversity; moreover, our experience with policy "czars" over the years has shown that this organizational approach does not lead to better or more integrated policy.

We should learn from the Internet itself—what is needed is better horizontal and networked coordination among all the affected agencies, with the White House playing a vital agenda-setting and convening role. For this reason, I also believe creating a separate cyber assistant secretary and cyber bureau at the State Department is a move in the wrong direction—we need to integrate innovative cyber policy into all bureaus, not balkanize it as one of many competing perspectives.

That is why former secretary of state Clinton created the position of cyber coordinator, a position I think should be strengthened as a part of the government-wide network for building and implementing good cyber policy.

James B. Steinberg
joined by Phoebe Yang

This is, on balance, an excellent report. The title gets it right: rather than joining today's narrow drumbeat on cybersecurity, this report emphasizes the Internet as a whole and the importance of maintaining its openness and security together. I would like to underscore two points arising from the report's treatment of this challenge.

First, an Internet that is both secure and open is a difficult balance to maintain, since regulation can be hard to achieve. No one state can singlehandedly alter the Internet's protocols and growth, and those that have tried are not good models; they tend not to embrace the rule of law, and they are deeply ambivalent about the global character of the Internet. To be sure, there is a role that regulation can play in improving the state of the Internet, and this report discusses efforts of the U.S. Congress in that area.

Such efforts are cautionary; legislation specifically and governmental intervention more generally in the area of Internet technology can be tricky. Although, for example, there are areas of the Computer Fraud and Abuse Act (CFAA) that could be updated to strengthen security, the CFAA has recently been rightly criticized for criminalizing a broad range of activities that should not qualify as criminal acts and may actually stifle legitimate security research. Efforts to reform the CFAA to clarify the actions that private-sector actors can take to protect networks should incorporate changes that limit criminal penalties for non-hacking activity. For example, CFAA reform could clarify current provisions to make clear that violations of a website's terms of service, while possibly a civil issue, should not be criminally prosecutable. Likewise, good-faith efforts to investigate security flaws should not be criminal acts.

I agree with the report's emphasis on market solutions, such as working with advertising networks, to mitigate the problem of sites built on infringing content, though elements of due process and the ability to appeal such decisions should not be eliminated merely because the solutions are private.

Second, the report includes mention of mutual-aid frameworks among approaches to Internet resilience. While not panaceas, these approaches show great promise. The Internet was built—and continues to work—thanks to the collective work of and cooperation among many individuals and firms. We should encourage the development of technologies that allow Internet users themselves, large and small, to contribute to its robustness. This can range from efforts to maintain access to content despite DDoS attacks to new kinds of ad hoc networks that can supplement traditional Internet access paths in the event of local overload or disruption during crises.

The interests of governments that embrace democracy, human and civil rights, and the free movement of ideas have been advanced by the past twenty years of Internet and Web development. With awareness of the real challenges that confront the continued success of the Internet and appreciation for the qualities that made the Internet thrive, this report helps sketch how to keep the Internet thriving.

Jonathan L. Zittrain
joined by Elana Berkowitz

Glossary

Anonymous: A loosely organized activist hacking group responsible for hacking government and other websites they consider to be symbols of authority.

ARPANET: A computer network considered to be the predecessor to the Internet, developed by the Advanced Research Project Agency (now the Defense Advanced Research Projects Agency) in the 1960s and 1970s as a means of communication between research laboratories and universities.

Botnet: A network of private computers infected with malicious software and controlled as a group, sometimes without the owners' knowledge.

Code: A text listing of commands to be compiled or assembled into an executable computer program.

Country code top-level domain (ccTLD): An Internet top-level domain generally used or reserved for a country, a sovereign state, or a dependent territory (for example, .il for Israel).

Cyber Intelligence Sharing and Protection Act (CISPA): A proposed law in the U.S. House of Representatives that would allow for the sharing of Internet traffic information between the U.S. government and certain technology and manufacturing companies. The stated aim of the bill is to help the U.S. government investigate cyber threats and ensure the security of networks against cyberattacks.

Distributed denial of service (DDoS) attack: An attempt to make a machine or network resource unavailable to its intended users by sending thousands of connection requests to a website every second.

Domain Name System (DNS): A hierarchical naming system for computers, services, or any resource connected to the Internet or a private network.

Domain Name System Security Extensions (DNSSEC): A proposed suite of Internet Engineering Task Force specifications for securing certain kinds of information provided by the Domain Name System (DNS) as used on Internet Protocol networks. It is a set of extensions to DNS that provide origin authentication of DNS data, authenticated denial of existence, and data integrity, but not availability or confidentiality.

Duqu: A malicious computer virus designed to gather intelligence data from entities such as industrial control manufacturers in order to be able to launch a future attack on an industrial control facility. Internet security specialists uncovered Duqu in October 2011, declaring that its code was nearly identical to that of an earlier computer worm called Stuxnet.

Fixed broadband: High-speed data transmission to homes and businesses using technologies such as T1, cable, DSL, and FiOS, excluding cellular data.

Flame: A malicious software discovered in 2012 that attacks computers running the Microsoft Windows operating system. The program is being used for targeted cyber espionage in Middle Eastern countries.

Generic top-level domain (gTLD): The core group of generic top-level domains, which consists of the .com, .info, .net, and .org domains.

Hacker: A person who uses computers to gain unauthorized access to data.

Hacktivist: A portmanteau of the words hacker and activist, used to connote a hacker who claims to have a political or philosophical agenda.

Honeypot: A trap set to detect, deflect, or in some manner counteract attempts at unauthorized use of information systems.

Information and communication technology (ICT): A specific kind of information technology that stresses the role of unified communications, including the integration of telecommunications and computers.

Information Sharing and Analysis Center (ISAC): A private-public institution created by the U.S. federal government that provides a forum for private-sector actors to share sector-specific threat and vulnerability information.

Information technology (IT): The use of computers and telecommunications equipment to store, retrieve, transmit, and manipulate data, often in the context of a business or other enterprise.

International Telecommunications Regulation (ITR): International rules for telecommunications, including international tariffs, set forth by the International Telecommunications Union.

International Telecommunications Union (ITU): A specialized agency of the United Nations responsible for issues that concern information and communication technologies.

Internet Engineering Task Force (IETF): A group of engineers who set voluntary standards for Internet engineering and identify best practices. Though the IETF has no mechanism for enforcement, the standards are default technical Internet requirements.

Internet Corporation for Assigned Names and Numbers (ICANN): A nonprofit organization that sets rules for creating and distributing domain names. It operates multilaterally from California.

Internet of things: A network that links sensors in physical objects, such as refrigerators and pacemakers, through virtual networks using Internet Protocol addresses.

Internet Protocol (IP) address: A numerical label assigned to every device participating in a computer network. The IP address is used to communicate between servers.

LulzSec: A small offshoot of hacker activist group Anonymous, Lulz Security (LulSec or LulzSec) hacks into company and government networks for political reasons.

Malware: Short for malicious software, or any software intended to damage or disable computers and computer systems.

Mutual Legal Assistance Treaties (MLAT): Agreements between nations to exchange information in support of investigations of criminal behavior.

Protect IP Act (PIPA): A bill introduced in the U.S. Senate to expand the ability of U.S. law enforcement to fight online trafficking in copyrighted intellectual property and counterfeit goods, which was defeated after popular protest. It is the Senate counterpart of the Stop Online Piracy Act (SOPA).

Red October: A malicious computer virus designed to gather intelligence from Russian-speaking public sector officials in the former Soviet Union and other countries, discovered in 2012.

Server: A computer or computer program that manages access to a centralized resource or service in a network.

Shamoon: A computer virus discovered in 2012 that was aimed at disrupting network access in the energy sector and destroyed thirty thousand computers in Saudi Aramco.

Social media: A means of interactions among people in which they create, share, and exchange information and ideas in virtual communities and networks (for example, Facebook and Twitter).

Stop Online Piracy Act (SOPA): A bill introduced in the U.S. House of Representatives to expand the ability of U.S. law enforcement to fight online trafficking in copyrighted intellectual property and counterfeit goods, which was defeated after popular protest. It is the House of Representatives counterpart to the Protect IP Act (PIPA).

Stuxnet: A computer worm discovered in June 2010 believed to have been created by the United States and Israel to attack Iran's nuclear facilities.

Top-level domain (TLD): The letters immediately following the final dot in an Internet address (for example, .org and .com).

United States Computer Emergency Readiness Team (U.S.-CERT): A clearinghouse for information on cyberattacks, threats, and vulnerabilities under the U.S. Department of Homeland Security.

Endnotes

1. "Remarks of the President on Securing Our Nation's Cyber Infrastructure," White House, May 29, 2009, http://www.whitehouse.gov/the_press_office/Remarks-by-the-President-on-Securing-Our-Nations-Cyber-Infrastructure.

2. Apps are special software on handheld devices that interact with Internet-based data services; "Information and Communications for Development: Maximizing Mobile," World Bank, 2012, http://siteresources.worldbank.org/EXTINFORMATIONAND-COMMUNICATIONANDTECHNOLOGIES/Resources/IC4D-2012-Report.pdf.

3. See Figure 1.28 in "OECD Internet Economy Outlook 2012," Organization for Economic Cooperation and Development, October 2012, p. 57.

4. "2013 Global R&D Funding Forecast," *R&D Magazine*, December 2012, http://www.rdmag.com/sites/rdmag.com/files/GFF2013Final2013_reduced.pdf, pp. 16–17, 31–32.

5. Matthieu Pélissié du Rausas, James Manyika, Eric Hazan, Jacques Bughin, Michael Chui, and Rémi Said, "Internet Matters: The Net's sweeping impact on growth, jobs, and prosperity." McKinsey Global Institute, May 2011, http://www.mckinsey.com/insights/mgi/research/technology_and_innovation/internet_matters.

6. Ibid.

7. Caroline Freund and Diana Weinhold, "The Internet and international trade in services." *American Economic Review*, vol. 92, no. 2, May 2002, pp. 236–40; George R.G. Clarke and Scott J. Wallsten, "Has the Internet Increased Trade? Developed and Developing Country Evidence," *Economic Inquiry*, vol. 44, no. 3, July 2006, pp. 465–84; "Toward a Single Global Digital Economy: The First Report of the Aspen Institute IDEA Project," Aspen Institute, 2012, http://www.aspeninstitute.org/sites/default/files/content/upload/IDEA_Project_Toward_a_Single_Global_Digital_Economy.pdf.

8. "The Economic Impact of Shutting Down Internet and Mobile Phone Services in Egypt," Organization for Economic Cooperation and Development, February 4, 2011, http://www.oecd.org/fr/pays/egypte/theeconomicimpactofshuttingdowninternetandmobilephoneservicesinegypt.htm.

9. "China Business Climate Survey Report," AmCham China, 2013, http://web.resource.amchamchina.org/cmsfile/2013/03/29/0640e5a7e0c8f86ff4a380150357bbef.pdf.

10. Lee Rainie, Aaron Smith, Kay Lehman Schlozman, Henry Brady, Sidney Verba, "Social Media and Political Engagement," Pew Research Center, October 19, 2012. http://pewinternet.org/Reports/2012/Political-Engagement.aspx.

11. Wolfgang Kleinwachter, "The History of Internet Governance," in "Governing the Internet: Freedom and Regulation in the OSCE Region," Organization for Security and Cooperation in Europe, 2007, http://www.osce.org/fom/26169.

12. Each Web address is made up of a series of characters separated by dots, such as www.cfr.org. The last label, .org, is referred to as a top-level domain name. These are the

highest-level names in the hierarchy and include country codes such as .il for Israel and generic names such as .com and .net. Other countries pushed for a more rapid adoption of different endings and to be able to use languages other than English; a growing number of internationalized domain names have been added for thirty-one countries and territories in the past two years.

13. The World Summit on the Information Society is jointly organized by UN Educational, Scientific and Cultural Organization, International Telecommunication Union, UN Conference on Trade and Development, and the UN Development Program.

14. The legislation threatened to weaken the universality of the Domain Name System, posed a significant risk of collateral damage by affecting users' ability to reach non-infringing Internet content, and undermined a critical component (Domain Name System Security Extensions or DNSSEC) of a wider cybersecurity strategy. Steve Crocker, David Dagon, Dan Kaminsky, Danny McPherson, Paul Vixie, "Security and Other Technical Concerns Raised by the DNS Filtering Requirements in the PROTECT IP Bill," May 2011, http://domainincite.com/docs/PROTECT-IP-Technical-Whitepaper-Final.pdf.

15. With the expansion of generic top-level domain names, .com and .org could be joined by over a thousand new endings, including .toyota, .baby, .islam, and .cloud.

16. Or 340,282,366,920,938,000,000,000,000,000,000,000. The current standard, IPv4, uses a 32-bit address space, IPv6 uses a 128-bit address space. Asia and Europe have already run out of v4. Small blocks remain in the Americas and Africa but are difficult to get.

17. "Norton Cybercrime Report," Symantec Corporation, 2012, http://us.norton.com/cybercrimereport/promo; "Cyber Security M&A: Decoding deals in the global Cyber Security industry," PricewaterhouseCoopers, November 2011, http://www.pwc.com/gx/en/aerospace-defence/publications/cyber-security-mergers-and-acquisitions.jhtml; Ross Anderson, Chris Barton, Rainer Böhme, Michel J.G. van Eeten, Michael Levi, Tyler Moore, Stefan Savage, "Measuring the Cost of Cybercrime," University of Cambridge, 2012, http://weis2012.econinfosec.org/papers/Anderson_WEIS2012.pdf.

18. Josh Rogin, "NSA Chief: Cybercrime constitutes the greatest transfer of wealth in history," ForeignPolicy.com, July 9, 2012, http://thecable.foreignpolicy.com/posts/2012/07/09/nsa_chief_cybercrime_constitutes_the_greatest_transfer_of_wealth_in_history.

19. Taylor Armerding, "Costly cyberespionage on 'relentless upward trend,'" CSO Online, December 18, 2012, http://www.csoonline.com/article/724228/costly-cyberespionage-on-relentless-upward-trend-.

20. Christ Strohm, Eric Engleman, and Dave Michaels, "Cyberattacks Abound Yet Companies Tell SEC Losses Are Few," Bloomberg, April 3, 2013, http://www.bloomberg.com/news/2013-04-04/cyberattacks-abound-yet-companies-tell-sec-losses-are-few.html.

21. The largest DDoS attack previously recorded was 100 gigabits per second (Gbps). The attack on Spamhaus was 300 Gbps at its peak; John Markoff and Nicole Perloth, "Firm Is Accused of Sending Spam, and Fight Jams Internet," New York Times, March 26, 2013, http://www.nytimes.com/2013/03/27/technology/internet/online-dispute-becomes-internet-snarling-attack.html.

22. James A. Lewis, "Conflict and Negotiation in Cyberspace," Center for Strategic and International Studies, February 2013, http://csis.org/files/publication/130208_Lewis_ConflictCyberspace_Web.pdf.

23. Leon E. Panetta, "Remarks by Secretary Panetta on Cybersecurity to the Business Executives for National Security, New York City," October 11, 2012, http://www.defense.gov/transcripts/transcript.aspx?transcriptid=5136.

24. Nicole Blake Johnson, "Report: Cyberattacks on critical infrastructure jump 383 percent in 2011," *Federal Times*, July 3, 2012, http://www.federaltimes.com/article/20120703/IT01/307030004/Report-Cyber-attacks-critical-infrastructure-jump-383-2011.

25. In written testimony to the Senate Intelligence Committee, Director of National Intelligence James R. Clapper Jr. said there was only a "remote chance" of "a major cyberattack against U.S. critical infrastructure systems during the next two years that would result in long-term, wide-scale disruption of services, such as a regional power outage. The level of technical expertise and operational sophistication required for such an attack—including the ability to create physical damage or overcome mitigation factors like manual overrides—will be out of reach for most actors during this time frame. Advanced cyber actors—such as Russia and China—are unlikely to launch such a devastating attack against the United States outside of a military conflict or crisis that they believe threatens their vital interests." James R. Clapper Jr., "Worldwide Threat Assessment of the U.S. Intelligence Community," testimony delivered before the Senate Select Committee on Intelligence, March 12, 2013, http://intelligence.senate.gov/130312/clapper.pdf.

26. "The National Strategy to Secure Cyberspace," United States Computer Emergency Readiness Team, February 2003, http://www.us-cert.gov/sites/default/files/publications/cyberspace_strategy.pdf.

27. "The Comprehensive National Cybersecurity Initiative," White House, http://www.whitehouse.gov/sites/default/files/cybersecurity.pdf.

28. "Cyberspace Policy Review: Assuring a Trusted and Resilient Information and Communications Infrastructure," White House, http://www.whitehouse.gov/assets/documents/Cyberspace_Policy_Review_final.pdf.

29. "International Strategy for Cyberspace: Prosperity, Security, and Openness in a Networked World," White House May 2011, http://www.whitehouse.gov/sites/default/files/rss_viewer/international_strategy_for_cyberspace.pdf.

30. Council of Europe, "Convention on Cybercrime CETS No. 185," http://conventions.coe.int/Treaty/Commun/ChercheSig.asp?NT=185&CM=&DF=&CL=ENG.

31. U.S. Department of Defense, "Department of Defense Strategy for Operating in Cyberspace," July 2011, http://www.defense.gov/news/d20110714cyber.pdf.

32. Hillary Rodham Clinton, "Remarks on Internet Freedom," speech delivered at the Newseum in Washington, DC, January 21, 2010, http://www.state.gov/secretary/rm/2010/01/135519.htm; "Internet Rights and Wrongs: Choices & Challenges in a Networked World," speech delivered at the George Washington University, February 15, 2011, http://www.state.gov/secretary/rm/2011/02/156619.htm; "Conference on Internet Freedom," speech delivered at Fokker Terminal in The Hague, Netherlands, December 8, 2011, http://www.state.gov/secretary/rm/2011/12/178511.htm.

33. Internet Freedom Fellows, "About the Internet Freedom Fellowship," http://www.internetfreedomfellows.com/about-the-internet-freedom-fellowship/.

34. National Telecommunications and Information Administration, "Internet Policy Task Force," http://www.ntia.doc.gov/category/internet-policy-task-force.

35. Anu Bradford, "The Brussels Effect," *Northwestern University Law Review*, vol. 107, no. 1, Fall 2012, pp. 1–68, http://www.law.northwestern.edu/lawreview/v107/n1/1/LR107n-1Bradford.pdf.

36. For example, after a six-year process that involved input from the business community, civil society, registries, registrars, and governments, ICANN approved the expansion of top-level domain names. Members of the Senate then called hearings on the expansion, and several called for a delay in the process.

37. In response to the proposed DNS filtering in SOPA/PIPA, different groups of software developers began to develop a next generation of DNS, one distributed much like a peer-to-peer network and thereby resistant to censorship.

38. Freedom Online Coalition, "Freedom Online: Joint Action for Free Expression on the Internet," November, 20, 2012, http://www.humanrights.gov/2012/11/20/freedom-online-joint-action-for-free-expression-on-the-internet/.

39. Moore's law observes that the number of transistors on an integrated circuit, and thus processing speed and memory capacity, doubles every two years.

40. "Defending the Networks: The NATO Policy on Cyber Defense," North Atlantic Treaty Organization, 2011, http://www.nato.int/nato_static/assets/pdf/pdf_2011_09/20111004_110914-policy-cyberdefence.pdf.

41. As Director of National Intelligence James R. Clapper Jr. said, "Cyber criminals also threaten U.S. economic interests. They are selling tools, via a growing black market, that might enable access to critical infrastructure systems or get into the hands of state and nonstate actors." Clapper, "Worldwide Threat Assessment of the U.S. Intelligence Community."

42. Richard A. Clarke, "Securing Cyberspace Through International Norms: Recommendations for Policymakers and the Private Sector," Good Harbor Security Risk Management, LLC, http://www.goodharbor.net/media/pdfs/SecuringCyberspace_web.pdf.

43. INTERPOL, "The INTERPOL Global Complex for Innovation," http://www.interpol.int/About-INTERPOL/The-INTERPOL-Global-Complex-for-Innovation.

44. For an example of how this might work, see Jonathan Zittrain, "A Mutual Aid Treaty for the Internet," Brookings Institution, January 27, 2011, http://www.brookings.edu/research/papers/2011/01/27-internet-treaty-zittrain.

45. World Economic Forum, "Partnering for Cyber Resilience (PCR)," http://www.weforum.org/issues/partnering-cyber-resilience-pcr.

46. General Alexander told the Senate Armed Services Committee that states would be deterred from launching a major electronic attack on vital infrastructure in the United States because "a devastating attack on the critical infrastructure and population of the United States by cyber means would be correctly traced back to its source and elicit a prompt and proportionate response." Keith B. Alexander, "Statement of General B. Keith Alexander before the Senate Committee on Armed Services," testimony delivered in Washington, DC, March 12, 2013, http://www.armed-services.senate.gov/statemnt/2013/03%20March/Alexander%2003-12-13.pdf.

47. Leon Panetta, "Remarks by Secretary Panetta on Cybersecurity to the Business Executives for National Security, New York City."

48. Under international law, it is widely (but not universally) accepted that states may respond in "anticipatory self-defense" against "imminent" threats. Traditionally, the notion of "imminent" generally referred to expected attacks that were temporally immediate, leaving no time to pursue other options than self-defense, but contemporary security threats have generated significant debate about appropriate criteria for evaluating whether the imminence threshold is met.

49. David E. Sanger, "Obama Order Sped Up Wave of Cyberattacks Against Iran," New York Times, June 1, 2012, http://www.nytimes.com/2012/06/01/world/middleeast/obama-ordered-wave-of-cyberattacks-against-iran.html; Ellen Nakashima, Greg Miller, and Julie Tate, "U.S., Israel Developed Flame Computer Virus to Slow Iranian Nuclear Efforts, Officials Say," Washington Post, June 19, 2012, http://articles.washingtonpost.com/2012-06-19/world/35460741_1_stuxnet-computer-virus-malware.

50. Andy Sullivan, "Obama Budget Makes Cybersecurity a Growing U.S. Priority," Reuters, April 10, 2013, http://www.reuters.com/article/2013/04/11/us-usa-fiscal-cybersecurity-idUSBRE93913S20130411.

51. Ellen Nakashima, "Pentagon to Boost Cybersecurity Force," Washington Post, January 27, 2013, http://www.washingtonpost.com/world/national-security/pentagon-to-boost-cybersecurity-force/2013/01/19/d87d9dc2-5fec-11e2-b05a-605528f6b712_story.html.

52. Ellen Nakashima, "Pentagon Creating Teams to Launch Cyberattacks as Threat Grows," *Washington Post*, March 12, 2013, http://articles.washingtonpost.com/2013-03-12/world/37645469_1_new-teams-national-security-threat-attacks.

53. Ellen Nakashima, "Obama Signs Secret Directive to Help Thwart Cyberattacks," *Washington Post*, November 14, 2012, http://articles.washingtonpost.com/2012-11-14/world/35505871_1_networks-cyberattacks-defense.

54. David E. Sanger and Thom Shanker, "Broad Powers Seen for Obama in Cyberstrikes," *New York Times*, February 3, 2013, http://www.nytimes.com/2013/02/04/us/broad-powers-seen-for-obama-in-cyberstrikes.html.

55. See, for example, General Alexander's statement: "Let me be clear, this defend-the-nation team is not a defensive team, this is an offensive team that the Department of Defense would use to defend the nation if it were attacked in cyberspace." Keith B. Alexander, "Statement of General B. Keith Alexander before the Senate Committee on Armed Services"; John Reed, "Cyber Command fielding 13 'offensive' cyber deterrence units," ForeignPolicy.com, March 12, 2013, http://killerapps.foreignpolicy.com/posts/2013/03/12/us_cyber_command_developing_13_offensive_cyber_deterrence_units.

56. Defense Science Board, "Task Force Report: Resilient Military Systems and the Advanced Cyber Threat," U.S. Department of Defense, January 2013, http://www.acq.osd.mil/dsb/reports/ResilientMilitarySystems.CyberThreat.pdf.

57. In 2004, the United States and UK declared in a submission to the UN secretary-general that international humanitarian law covered the use of information and communication technologies; Harold Hongju Koh, "International Law in Cyberspace," speech delivered at the USCYBERCOM Inter-Agency Legal Conference in Ft. Meade, MD, September 18, 2012, http://www.state.gov/s/l/releases/remarks/197924.htm.

58. The GGE is working as part of the First Committee on Disarmament and International Security of the UN General Assembly.

59. NATO Cooperative Cyber Defence Centre of Excellence, "The Tallinn Manual," https://www.ccdcoe.org/249.html.

60. Nicole Perloth, David E. Sanger, and Michael S. Schmidt, "As Hacking Against U.S. Rises, Experts Try to Pin Down Motive," *New York Times*, March 3, 2013, http://www.nytimes.com/2013/03/04/us/us-weighs-risks-and-motives-of-hacking-by-china-or-iran.html.

61. "Foreign Spies Stealing US Economic Secrets in Cyberspace: Report to Congress on Foreign Economic Collection and Industrial Espionage, 2009-2011," Office of the National Counterintelligence Executive, October 2011, http://www.ncix.gov/publications/reports/fecie_all/Foreign_Economic_Collection_2011.pdf.

62. "Administration Strategy on Mitigating the Theft of U.S. Trade Secrets," White House, February 2013, http://www.whitehouse.gov//sites/default/files/omb/IPEC/admin_strategy_on_mitigating_the_theft_of_u.s._trade_secrets.pdf.

63. Susan Heavey, "Cyber threats against U.S. 'ramping up,' Obama says." Reuters, March 13, 2013, http://in.reuters.com/article/2013/03/13/usa-obama-cyber-threat-idINDEE92C0A220130313.

64. U.S. State Department, "Proliferation Security Initiative," http://www.state.gov/t/isn/c10390.htm.

65. nCircle, "Black Hat Survey: 36% of Information Security Professionals Have Engaged in Retaliatory Hacking," http://www.ncircle.com/index.php?s=news_press_2012_07-26-Black-Hat-Survey-36-percent-of-Information-Security-Professionals-Have-Engaged-in-Retaliatory-Hacking.

66. Nicole Blake Johnson, "Report Shows Gaps in Cyber Workforce," *Federal Times*, April 4, 2013, http://www.federaltimes.com/article/20130404/IT01/304040001/Report-shows-gaps-cyber-workforce.

67. Jim Finkle and Noel Randewich, "Experts Warn of Shortage of U.S. Cyber Pros," Reuters, June 13, 2012, http://www.reuters.com/article/2012/06/13/us-media-tech-summit-symantec-idUSBRE85B1E220120613.

68. Homeland Security Advisory Council, "Cyberskills Task Force Report," U.S. Department of Homeland Security, Fall 2012, http://www.dhs.gov/sites/default/files/publications/HSAC%20CyberSkills%20Report%20-%20Final.pdf.

69. Cyber Warrior Act of 2013, S 658, 113th Cong., Section 3a.

70. William Jefferson Clinton, "Presidential Decision Directive 63: Critical Infrastructure Protection," May 1998, http://www.fas.org/irp/offdocs/pdd/pdd-63.htm.

71. Executive Order no. 13636, *Federal Register* 78, no. 2 (February 19, 2013).

72. One positive trend to note is that U.S.-CERT has the growing ability to map the IP addresses for botnets used in DDoS attacks and provide advance warning of coming attacks and technical data necessary for the private sector to block attacks on its own.

73. U.S. Department of Homeland Security, "Cyber Storm: Securing Cyber Space," http://www.dhs.gov/cyber-storm-securing-cyber-space.

74. "European Union-United States Trade Principles for Information and Communication Technology Services," April 4, 2011, http://trade.ec.europa.eu/doclib/docs/2011/april/tradoc_147780.pdf; OECD, "Communique on Principles for Internet Policy-Making," June 28-29, 2011, http://www.oecd.org/internet/innovation/48289796.pdf; National Foreign Trade Council, "Promoting Cross-Border Data Flows: Priorities for the Business Community," http://www.nftc.org/default/Innovation/PromotingCrossBorderDataFlowsNFTC.pdf; "Toward a Single Global Digital Economy: The First Report of the Aspen Institute IDEA Project," Aspen Institute.

75. "Written Ministerial Statement: Data Protection," UK Ministry of Justice, November 22, 2012, http://www.parliament.uk/documents/commons-vote-office/November_2012/22-11-12/7-Justice-DataProtection.pdf.

76. "The right to be forgotten—between expectations and practice," European Network and Information Security Agency, November 20, 2012, https://www.enisa.europa.eu/activities/identity-and-trust/library/deliverables/the-right-to-be-forgotten.

77. "Bridging the Skills Gap: Help Wanted, Skills Packing: Why the Mismatch in Today's Economy?" ATSD, October 2012, http://nist.gov/mep/upload/Bridging-the-Skills-Gap_2012.pdf.

78. Microsoft, "Technology Analysts Predict Widening Cloud Skills Gap for IT," December 19, 2012, http://www.microsoft.com/en-us/news/Press/2012/Dec12/12-19CloudSkillsPR.aspx.

79. Vivek Wadhwa, AnnaLee Saxenian, Ben Rissing, and Gary Gereffi, "America's New Immigrant Entrepreneurs," University of California, Berkeley, School of Information, January 4, 2007, http://people.ischool.berkeley.edu/~anno/Papers/Americas_new_immigrant_entrepreneurs_I.pdf; Vivek Wadhwa, AnnaLee Saxenian, and F. Daniel Siciliano, "Then and Now: America's New Immigrant Entrepreneurs, Part VII, October 2012, http://www.kauffman.org/uploadedFiles/Then_and_now_americas_new_immigrant_entrepreneurs.pdf.

80. "Internet Governance Forum," http://www.intgovforum.org/cms/.

81. "Open Government Partnership," http://www.opengovpartnership.org/.

82. "The promotion, protection and enjoyment of human rights on the Internet," in "Report of the Human Rights Council on Its Twentieth Session," Human Rights Council, August 3, 2012, http://www.ohchr.org/Documents/HRBodies/HRCouncil/RegularSession/Session20/A-HRC-20-2_en.pdf.

83. Hillary Rodham Clinton, "Internet Rights and Wrongs: Choices & Challenges in a Networked World," speech delivered at George Washington University, February 15, 2011, http://www.state.gov/secretary/rm/2011/02/156619.htm.

84. "Global Network Initiative," http://www.globalnetworkinitiative.org.
85. John Markoff, "Rights Group Reports on Abuses of Surveillance and Censorship Technology," *New York Times*, January 16, 2013, http://www.nytimes.com/2013/01/16/business/rights-group-reports-on-abuses-of-surveillance-and-censorship-technology.html.

Task Force Members

Elana Berkowitz currently works at Etsy, building their international business, and is an adjunct fellow at the New America Foundation's Open Technology Initiative. Previously, she was an engagement manager at McKinsey and Company, where she primarily supported technology and telecommunications clients in emerging markets. She served in two posts in the Obama administration, as innovation adviser in the office of Secretary Clinton at the State Department and as the economic opportunity director for the National Broadband Plan at the Federal Communications Commission. Prior to graduate school, she was part of the founding team of Campus Progress, a national organization that builds the next generation of progressive youth leaders on campuses, in their communities, and online; it is part of the Center for American Progress. Berkowitz completed a joint MBA and MPA at Harvard Business School and Harvard Kennedy School, where she was a Zuckerman fellow.

Bob Boorstin is a director of public policy in the Washington, DC, office of Google, Inc., where he has developed the company's work on the global promotion of online free expression and works on a wide range of domestic and international issues. He has more than twenty years of experience in national security, political communications, public opinion research, and journalism. During the Clinton administration, he served in the National Security Council as the president's chief foreign policy speechwriter and later advised the secretaries of treasury and state. Prior to coming to Google, Boorstin established and ran the national security programs at the Center for American Progress, a leading Washington think tank. He has advised Fortune 500 companies and some of the nation's leading advocacy groups, and worked on more than a dozen political campaigns in the United States and abroad. Early in his career, he was a reporter for the *New York Times* and other publications.

Jeff A. Brueggeman is vice president of public policy and deputy chief privacy officer for AT&T. In this role, he is responsible for developing and coordinating AT&T's public policy positions on privacy, cyber-security, and Internet issues. He leads the team that manages AT&T's privacy policies and provides guidance on data privacy and security issues. His team also supports AT&T's business in the operation of its global Internet network and deployment of cloud computing and other emerging services. Brueggeman participates in a wide range of legislative, regulatory, and policy development proceedings involving privacy, cybersecurity, and Internet issues. In addition, he represents AT&T in various international events and organizations related to Internet governance, including the Internet Governance Forum and ICANN. Prior to joining AT&T, Brueggeman worked as a telecommunications attorney in private practice.

Peter Cleveland is vice president of legal and corporate affairs and responsible for global public policy at Intel Corporation. He oversees a team of attorneys and policy professionals responsible for establishing favorable laws, regulations, and policies to enable Intel's global business success. Cleveland acts as the company's public policy liaison to foreign governments and regulatory bodies as well as the U.S. Congress and Obama administration in Washington, DC. He represents Intel on the boards of various trade associations and related organizations, including the Information Technology Industry Council, the Transatlantic Business Council, the Center for International Private Enterprise, the National Association of Manufacturers, and the National Committee on United States-China Relations. Cleveland joined Intel in 2008 from the office of California senator Dianne Feinstein, where he served as chief of staff. Previously, he worked as an attorney for a leading international law firm. He received his undergraduate degree from Columbia University in 1987 and his law degree from Georgetown University in 1997. He is a member of the New York and the District of Columbia Bars and of the Council on Foreign Relations.

Esther Dyson is chairman of EDventure Holdings. Her primary activity is investing in and nurturing start-ups, with a recent focus on health care and aerospace. In policy, she is an active board member of the Sunlight Foundation, an advocate for government transparency, and of StopBadware.org, a pragmatic, corporate-funded organization that attempts to do just that by sharing information about specific threats and remedies. She was chairman of the Electronic Frontier Foundation for several years in the 1990s, and later became (nonexecutive) founding chairman of ICANN from 1998 to 2000. In business, her security investments have included PGP Inc., Sana Security (Company 51), and Cognitive Security. She is currently an investor in and sits on the advisory board of AnchorFree, creator of the Hotspot Shield private VPN tool. More generally, she is an active board member for WPP Group and a variety of start-ups, including 23andMe, Eventful, IBS Group (advisory board), Meetup, NewspaperDirect, Voxiva, and Yandex. Her past investments have included Medstory and Powerset (sold to Microsoft), Flickr and del.icio.us (sold to Yahoo!), and Brightmail (sold to Symantec). Her current investments include Factual Inc., GoodData, Singly, and many other start-ups.

Martha Finnemore is university professor of political science and international affairs at George Washington University in Washington, DC. Her research focuses on global governance, international organizations, ethics, and social theory. She is the coauthor, along with Michael Barnett, of *Rules for the World: International Organizations in Global Politics*, which won the International Studies Association's award for best book in 2006. She is also author of *National Interests in International Society* and *The Purpose of Intervention*, which won the American Political Science Association's Woodrow Wilson Award as "the best book published on government, politics, or international affairs" in 2004. Her most recent books are *Back to Basics: State Power in a Contemporary World* and *Who Governs the Globe?* Her articles have appeared in *International Organization, World Politics, Annual Review of Political Science, Review of International Studies, Review of International Political Economy*, and elsewhere. She is a fellow of the American Academy of Arts and Sciences, has been a visiting research fellow at the Brookings Institution and Stanford University, and has received fellowships or grants from the MacArthur Foundation, the Social Science Research Council, the Smith Richardson Foundation, and the United States Institute of Peace.

Patrick Gorman served as chief information security officer at Bank of America. He led the team responsible for the bank's information security strategy, policy, and program. Gorman is a senior strategy and technology executive with more than twenty-five years of experience in government and the private sector, including serving as associate director of national intelligence and chief information officer in the Office of the Director of National Intelligence. Before joining the bank, he was senior executive adviser for cybersecurity and advanced analytics at Booz Allen Hamilton, responsible for strategic planning and capability development for the firm's cybersecurity portfolio. He rejoined Booz Allen Hamilton from the Office of Director of National Intelligence, where he managed the Intelligence Community's Incident Response Center. Prior to Booz Allen Hamilton, Gorman spent ten years in the U.S. Air Force in the Electronic Security Command, Air Force Intelligence, and Air Force Special Operations Command on assignments for the National Security Agency's Central Security Service, the cryptologic support arm for the Department of Defense. Gorman serves on the advisory council of the BITS Financial Services Roundtable.

Michael V. Hayden is the former director of the National Security Agency and Central Intelligence Agency. As director of the Central Intelligence Agency, Hayden was responsible for overseeing the collection of information concerning the plans, intentions, and capabilities of the United States' adversaries; producing timely analysis for decision-makers; and conducting covert operations to thwart terrorists and other enemies of the United States. Before becoming director of the CIA, Hayden served as the country's first principal deputy director of national intelligence and was the highest-ranking intelligence officer in the armed forces. Earlier, he served as director of the National Security Agency. Currently, he serves as a principal at the Chertoff Group, a security and risk management advisory firm, and as a distinguished visiting professor at George Mason University.

Eugene J. Huang is vice president of strategy and planning for the Enterprise Growth Group at American Express. He is also a visiting scholar in the Center for Technology Innovation at the Brookings Institution. Between 2006 and 2011, Huang served in a number of senior roles in the White House, the U.S. Treasury Department, the Consumer Financial Protection Bureau, and the Federal Communications Commission. In these roles, Huang was responsible for a wide range of policy initiatives, including international technology and innovation policy, the government operations and civic engagement chapters of the

U.S. national broadband plan, and international economic and finance policy with a specific emphasis on U.S. bilateral relations with China. Huang was also a White House fellow between 2006 and 2007, serving as an adviser to Secretary of the Treasury Henry M. Paulson. From 2002 to 2006, he served the Commonwealth of Virginia under Governor Mark R. Warner as the secretary of technology and previously as the deputy secretary of technology. Huang is a member of the board of the 100,000 Strong Foundation, a term member of the Council on Foreign Relations, a member of the International Institute for Strategic Studies, and a named inventor on two patents.

Anthony P. Lee is a general partner of Altos Ventures, a growth-stage venture capital fund investing in technology companies globally. He currently serves on the boards of several private technology companies. Prior to joining Altos, Lee was a marketing executive for two software companies and began his career at McKinsey & Company. Lee is board chair of TechSoup Global, the world's largest nonprofit technology distribution network, serving civil society organizations in more than forty countries. He is a member of the Pacific Council on International Policy and has served as a term member of the Council on Foreign Relations. He is also a cofounder of C100, the leading network for Canadian entrepreneurship, and a founding member of Full Circle Fund, a venture philanthropy group based in San Francisco. Lee graduated from Princeton University with an AB in politics and holds an MBA from Stanford University's Graduate School of Business. He was born in Canada and has worked and lived throughout Africa, Asia, Europe, and the Middle East.

Catherine B. Lotrionte is the director of the Institute for Law, Science and Global Security and visiting assistant professor of government and foreign service at Georgetown University. In 2006, she founded the CyberProject at Georgetown University under the auspices of the institute. Lotrionte and the institute focus on the role of international and domestic law and policy in recent and upcoming developments in cyber technology and cyber threats. In 2002, she was appointed by General Brent Scowcroft to be counsel to the President's Foreign Intelligence Advisory Board at the White House, a position she held until 2006. In 2002, she served as a legal counsel for the Joint Inquiry Committee of the Senate Select Committee on Intelligence. Prior to that, Lotrionte was assistant general counsel with the Office of General Counsel at the Central Intelligence Agency, where she provided legal advice relating to information warfare, foreign intelligence and counterintelligence activities, and international terrorism. Lotrionte earned her PhD from Georgetown University and her JD from New York University. She is the author of numerous publications, including two forthcoming books concerning U.S. national security law in the post–Cold War era and *Cyber Policy: An Instrument of International Relations, Intelligence and National Power*.

Susan Markham Lyne is CEO of the AOL Brand Group, where she oversees AOL's core experiences—AOL.com, AOL Mail, the AOL client, and AIM—as well as the suite of AOL's content brands, including TechCrunch, Engadget, SytleList, Patch, Moviefone, and MapQuest. Lyne was most recently chairman of Gilt Groupe, the innovative e-commerce company that pioneered "flash sales" in the United States. Prior to that, she served as president and CEO of Martha Stewart Living Omnimedia, where she led the company's recovery and return to profitability. From 1996 to 2004, Lyne held various positions at the Walt Disney Company and ABC, including executive vice president, development and new business; and executive vice president, movies and miniseries. Lyne spent fifteen years in the magazine industry before joining Disney. She was managing editor of *New Times* and the *Village Voice* and, in 1987, created and launched *Premiere* magazine, where she served as editor in chief and publication director. Lyne serves on the board of directors for Starz LLC and as vice chairman of the board of directors at Gilt Groupe. Lyne is a trustee of Rockefeller University and the New School and a member of the Council on Foreign Relations.

Naotaka Matsukata brings both public- and private-sector experience to his position as chief executive officer and president of FairWinds Partners, LLC. FairWinds is the largest provider of application and strategic services to Fortune 500 companies for ICANN's New gTLD Program. FairWinds works specifically with clients to optimize their use of the address bar and to help brands manage their online presence. Before FairWinds, Matsukata counseled global corporations on international trade and policy issues. He represented clients on major international trade disputes between the United States and the European Union and on some of the largest cross-border private equity transactions to date.

Matsukata's public service includes stints as a senior policy adviser on presidential campaigns, for a U.S. senator, and for the U.S. trade representative. He represented the United States in the Doha round of trade negotiations, the Kyoto Protocol talks on climate change, and in other critical multilateral policy negotiations. He is an adjunct professor at Johns Hopkins University's School for Advanced International Studies and has published widely in major Asian, European, and North American media outlets. He holds a PhD in history from Harvard University.

Jeff Moss is the chief security officer for the Internet Corporation for Assigned Names and Numbers. ICANN is a nonprofit corporation created in 1998 with responsibility for the security, stability, and resiliency of the global unique identifiers of the Internet. Moss is also the founder of both the Black Hat Briefings and DEF CON conferences that focus on cutting-edge information security research and convene more than ten thousand people a year. Before creating the Black Hat Briefings, Moss was a director at Secure Computing Corporation, where he helped establish its professional services department. His primary work was security assessments of large multinational corporations in the United States and Asia Pacific. Moss has also worked for Ernst & Young, LLP in its ISS division. Moss is currently a member of the U.S. Department of Homeland Security Advisory Council, providing advice and recommendations to the secretary of the Department of Homeland Security on matters related to homeland security. He is also a member of the Council on Foreign Relations. Moss graduated with a BA in criminal justice from Gonzaga University.

Craig James Mundie is senior adviser to Steve Ballmer, CEO of Microsoft Corporation. In this role, he works on major strategic projects within the company, as well as with government and business leaders around the world on technology policy, regulation, and standards. Previously, Mundie served as Microsoft's chief research and strategy officer, where he oversaw Microsoft Research, one of the world's largest computer science research organizations, and was responsible for Microsoft's long-term technology strategy, directing a number of technology incubations. For more than a decade, Mundie has been Microsoft's principal technology-policy liaison to the U.S. and foreign governments, with an emphasis on China, India, and Russia. He has served on the U.S. National Security Telecommunications Advisory

Committee and the Markle Foundation task force on national security
in the information age. In April 2009, Mundie was appointed by President Barack Obama to the President's Council of Advisers on Science
and Technology.

John D. Negroponte joined McLarty Associates as vice chairman
in 2009, following a distinguished career in diplomacy and national
security. He has been ambassador to Honduras, Mexico, the Philip-
pines, the United Nations, and Iraq. In Washington, he served twice
on the National Security Council staff, first as director for Vietnam in
the Nixon administration and then as deputy national security adviser
under President Reagan. He has also held a cabinet-level position as the
first director of national intelligence under President George W. Bush.
His most recent position in government was as deputy secretary of
state, where he served as the State Department's chief operating officer.
While in the private sector from 1997 to 2001, Negroponte was executive vice president of the McGraw-Hill Companies, responsible for
overseeing the company's international activities. During those years
he was also chairman of the French-American Foundation. In 2009,
Negroponte began a part-time position at his alma mater, Yale University, as a distinguished senior research fellow in grand strategy and as
a lecturer in international affairs. Negroponte serves as chairman of
the Council of the Americas/Americas Society and as a trustee of the
Asia Society. He is also co-chairman of the U.S.-Philippines Society, a
member of the Secretary of State's Foreign Affairs Policy Board, and
chairman of the Intelligence and National Security Alliance.

Joseph S. Nye Jr. is university distinguished service professor and former
dean of the Harvard Kennedy School. He received his BA summa cum
laude from Princeton University, won a Rhodes scholarship to Oxford,
and earned a PhD in political science from Harvard. He has served as
assistant secretary of defense for international security affairs, chair of
the National Intelligence Council, and a deputy undersecretary of state.
His most recent books include *Soft Power*, *The Powers to Lead*, and *The
Future of Power*. He is a fellow of the American Academy of Arts and Sciences, the British Academy, and the American Academy of Diplomacy.
In a recent survey of international relations scholars, he was ranked as
the most influential scholar on American foreign policy, and in 2011, *Foreign Policy* named him one of the top 100 Global Thinkers.

Samuel J. Palmisano was chairman, president, and chief executive officer of IBM Corporation from January 2003 through December 2011, and was senior adviser to IBM until his retirement on December 1, 2012. He was chairman of the board from January through September 2012. Under his leadership, IBM achieved record financial performance, transformed itself into a globally integrated enterprise, and introduced its Smarter Planet agenda. In a thirty-nine-year career with the company, Palmisano held leadership positions that included senior vice president and group executive of the Personal Systems Group, senior vice president and group executive of IBM Global Services, senior vice president and group executive of Enterprise Systems, and president and chief operating officer. Among his many business accomplishments, Palmisano was awarded two honorary doctor of humane letters degrees: from his alma mater Johns Hopkins University in 2012 and from Rensselaer Polytechnic Institute in 2005. In 2006, he was awarded an honorary fellowship from the London Business School. Palmisano has received a number of business awards, including the Atlantic Council's Distinguished Business Leadership Award in 2009 and the inaugural Deming Cup, presented in 2010 by the W. Edwards Deming Center for Quality, Productivity, and Competitiveness at Columbia Business School. He is also an elected member of the American Academy of Arts and Sciences and served as co-chair of the Council on Competitiveness's National Innovation Initiative.

Neal A. Pollard is a director in the forensics technology practice at PricewaterhouseCoopers, where he focuses on forensic investigations of cyber crime, economic espionage, and insider threats. He is also adjunct professor at Georgetown University. Previously, as a senior officer in the intelligence community, he served multiple managerial and operational counterterrorism assignments in the National Counterterrorism Center, the Office of the Director of National Intelligence, and the Central Intelligence Agency. He was director for counterterrorism on the staff of the U.S. Commission on the Prevention of Weapons of Mass Destruction Proliferation and Terrorism and was a member of the United Nation's Expert Working Group on use of the Internet for terrorist purposes. Before his government service, he was vice president of Hicks & Associates and general counsel and board director of the Terrorism Research Center, a corporation he cofounded in 1996. He holds a number of academic affiliations, including senior fellow of the Cyber Statecraft Initiative at the Atlantic Council, senior associate at the Center for Strategic and International Studies, and board director of the Cyber Conflict Studies Association. He is a member of the Council on Foreign Relations, where he was an international affairs fellow, and is a member of the Virginia Bar.

Elliot J. Schrage is the vice president of global communications and public policy at Facebook, where he is responsible for developing and coordinating important messages about products, corporate business, and partnerships. He also oversees the company's public policy strategy worldwide. Elliot joined Facebook from Google, where he was the vice president of communications and public affairs. He helped broaden and coordinate the company's messaging from a focus on product public relations to include all aspects of corporate, financial, policy, philanthropic, and internal communications. Earlier in his career, Elliot was the Bernard L. Schwarz senior fellow in business and foreign policy at the Council on Foreign Relations, senior vice president of global affairs for Gap, and an adjunct professor at Columbia University and Columbia Law School. Elliot holds a BA from Harvard University, an MA in public policy from the Harvard Kennedy School, and a JD from Harvard Law School.

Adam M. Segal is the Maurice R. Greenberg senior fellow for China studies at the Council on Foreign Relations. An expert on security issues, technology development, and Chinese domestic and foreign policy, Segal currently leads the Cyberconflict and Cybersecurity Initiative. His recent book *Advantage: How American Innovation Can Overcome the Asian Challenge* looks at the technological rise of Asia. Before coming to CFR, Segal was an arms control analyst for the China Project at the Union of Concerned Scientists. There, he wrote about missile defense, nuclear weapons, and Asian security issues. He has been a visiting scholar at the Massachusetts Institute of Technology's Center for International Studies, the Shanghai Academy of Social Sciences, and Tsinghua University in Beijing. He has taught at Vassar College and Columbia University. Segal is the author of *Digital Dragon: High-Technology Enterprises in China*, as well as several articles and book chapters on Chinese technology policy. His work has appeared in the *Economist, Financial Times, Foreign Policy, Wall Street Journal,* and *Foreign Affairs*, among others. He currently writes for the CFR blog Asia

Unbound. Segal has a BA and a PhD in government from Cornell University and an MA in international relations from Tufts University's Fletcher School of Law and Diplomacy.

Anne-Marie Slaughter is currently the Bert G. Kerstetter '66 university professor of politics and international affairs at Princeton University. Beginning in September 2013, she will assume the presidency of the New America Foundation and will become a professor emerita at Princeton. From 2009 to 2011, she served as director of policy planning for the U.S. Department of State, the first woman to hold that position. Upon leaving the State Department, she received the secretary's Distinguished Service Award for her work leading the Quadrennial Diplomacy and Development Review, as well as meritorious service awards from USAID and the Supreme Allied Commander for Europe. Before her government service, Slaughter was dean of Princeton's Woodrow Wilson School of Public and International Affairs from 2002 to 2009 and the J. Sinclair Armstrong professor of international, foreign, and comparative law at Harvard Law School from 1994 to 2002. Slaughter has written or edited six books and more than a hundred scholarly articles. *Foreign Policy* named her to its annual list of the top 100 global thinkers in 2009, 2010, 2011, and 2012. She received a BA from Princeton, an MPhil and a DPhil in international relations from Oxford, where she was a Daniel M. Sachs scholar, and a JD from Harvard.

James B. Steinberg is dean of the Maxwell School at Syracuse University and university professor of social science, international affairs, and law. Before becoming dean, he was deputy secretary of state, serving as the principal deputy to Secretary Hillary Clinton. From 2005 to 2008, Steinberg was dean of the Lyndon B. Johnson School of Public Affairs. From 2001 to 2005, Steinberg was vice president and director of foreign policy studies at the Brookings Institution, where he supervised a wide-ranging research program on U.S. foreign policy. Steinberg served as deputy national security adviser to President Bill Clinton from 1996 to 2000. During that period, he also served as the president's personal representative to the 1998 and 1999 G8 summits. Before becoming deputy national security adviser, Steinberg served as director of the State Department's policy planning staff and as deputy assistant secretary for analysis in the Bureau of Intelligence and Research. Previously, Steinberg was Senator Edward Kennedy's principal aide for the Senate

Armed Services Committee and minority counsel, U.S. Senate Labor and Human Resources Committee. Steinberg's most recent book is *Difficult Transitions: Foreign Policy Troubles at the Outset of Presidential Power* with Kurt M. Campbell. Steinberg received his BA from Harvard and a JD from Yale Law School.

Lawrence P. Tu serves as senior vice president and general counsel for Dell. In this role, he oversees the global legal department. He also manages government affairs and compliance and ethics functions. Previously, Tu was executive vice president and general counsel at NBC Universal, one of the world's fastest-growing and most profitable media and entertainment companies. He served in the same capacity at NBC for three years before that. Earlier, he was a partner at O'Melveny & Myers LLP, where he focused on energy, technology, Internet, and media-related transactions, including five years as managing partner of the Hong Kong office. Tu was also general counsel Asia-Pacific for Goldman Sachs, an attorney for the U.S. State Department, and a clerk for U.S. Supreme Court Justice Thurgood Marshall. Tu earned AB and JD degrees from Harvard University, as well as a bachelor's degree from Oxford University, where he was a Rhodes scholar.

Ernest James Wilson III is Walter Annenberg chair in communication and dean of the Annenberg School for Communication and Journalism at the University of Southern California. He is a professor of political science, a university fellow at the USC Center on Public Diplomacy at the Annenberg School, member of the board of the Pacific Council on International Policy and the National Academies' Computer Science and Telecommunications Board, and a member of the American Academy of Arts and Sciences. He served on the board of the Corporation for Public Broadcasting from 2000 to 2010, the last year as chairman. Wilson's experience at the intersection of communication and public policy spans the private and public sectors. He has served as a consultant to international agencies such as the World Bank and the United Nations, worked in government at the White House National Security Council and the Corporation for Public Broadcasting, and led research centers and academic departments at premier institutions of higher education. Wilson's current work concentrates on China-Africa relations, global sustainable innovation in high-technology industries, and the role of politics in the diffusion of information and communication technologies.

Phoebe Yang is managing director on communications and health-care technologies at Rock Water Ventures, LLC, where she advises investors, health-care providers, and entrepreneurs on growth strategies, and she serves as managing director of special projects for the CEO at The Advisory Board Company, where she has also led corporate and acquisitions strategy. Previously, she served as senior adviser to the chairman on broadband and general counsel of the National Broadband Plan Task Force at the Federal Communications Commission. She was vice president of corporate strategy and development and vice president of digital media at Discovery Communications LLC, as well as vice president of international strategy and policy at AOL Time Warner. She served as special coordinator for China rule of law under President Clinton and practiced corporate law at Hogan & Hartson, LLP after serving as law clerk to U.S. District Court for the Northern District of California judge William Schwarzer. Yang graduated Phi Beta Kappa with a BA in government and foreign affairs from the University of Virginia. She received her JD from Stanford Law School, where she was president and editor in chief of the *Stanford Law Review*.

Jonathan L. Zittrain is professor of law at Harvard Law School and the Harvard Kennedy School, professor of computer science at the Harvard School of Engineering and Applied Sciences, and cofounder of the Berkman Center for Internet & Society. His research interests include battles for control of digital property and content, cryptography, electronic privacy, the roles of intermediaries within Internet architecture, human computing, and the useful and unobtrusive deployment of technology in education. He performed the first large-scale tests of Internet filtering in China and Saudi Arabia, and as part of the OpenNet Initiative, coedited a series of studies of Internet filtering by national governments. His 2008 book *The Future of the Internet—And How to Stop It* is available from Yale University Press and Penguin UK, and under a Creative Commons license. He is a member of the board of directors of the Electronic Frontier Foundation and the board of advisers for *Scientific American*. He has served as a trustee of the Internet Society, as a Forum Fellow of the World Economic Forum, which named him a Young Global Leader, and as distinguished scholar in residence at the FCC, where he chairs the open Internet advisory committee.

Task Force Observers

Elana Broitman, during the course of the Task Force, served as the senior adviser to Senator Kirsten Gillibrand, supporting her on the Senate Armed Services Committee; on foreign policy matters during the senator's time on the Senate Foreign Relations Committee; and with cybersecurity legislation and policy. Broitman wrote and managed inclusion of cybersecurity provisions in the National Defense Authorization Act and the Senate's omnibus cybersecurity legislation. She worked with a number of New York State academic and business institutions in the nanotechnology, anticounterfeiting, directed energy, and rare earth sectors. Broitman's prior government experience includes serving as counsel to the House Foreign Affairs Committee and senior rule of law adviser for Europe and newly independent states at USAID. In the private sector, Broitman worked at Register.com, a leading domain name registrar, where she testified before the House Commerce and Judiciary committees regarding intellectual property and Internet policy, as well as the European Commission regarding Internet competition. She also represented the company at ICANN. Prior to that, Broitman worked in international policy at Pfizer, focusing on intellectual property matters in the Asian and European markets. Broitman began her career as an antitrust and corporate attorney with Arnold & Porter.

Zoe Baird is president of the Markle Foundation. Baird has led Markle's collaborative efforts to deploy information technology to reform the intelligence community to meet current threats and to catalyze improvements in health care. Previously, she initiated Markle's work with the UN and others to expand Internet access in developing countries and to build global Internet governance institutions like ICANN. She is currently leading a new initiative to expand middle-class economic security in a networked world. Baird was appointed by the president to the President's Foreign Intelligence Advisory Board (1994–2000), the G8 Heads of State Digital Opportunity Task Force (2000–2002), the Congressional Commission on the Roles and Capabilities of the U.S. Intelligence Community (1995); by the secretary of defense to his Technology and Policy Advisory Committee (2003–2004); and by the director of the National Security Agency and Cyber Command to the NSA Advisory Board Cyber Awareness and Response Panel (2010–2011). She has served as associate counsel to the president (1980–81), senior vice president and general counsel of Aetna, and a partner in O'Melveny & Myers. She holds an AB Phi Beta Kappa from the University of California, Berkeley, and a JD from the University of California, Berkeley, School of Law.

James P. Dougherty is an adjunct senior fellow at the Council on Foreign Relations in the Maurice R. Greenberg Center for Geoeconomic Studies. He has almost thirty years of diverse operating experiences in both IT and information services as CEO. He has produced turnarounds, taken companies public, successfully sold companies, and raised substantial private equity in one of the worst markets in twenty-five years. Dougherty's career began at Lotus Development, where he became the general manager of the Internet division and a member of the executive committee at the time of the company's sale to IBM. He then produced four consecutive turnarounds for investors—IntraLinks, Gartner, Prodigy, and MataMatrix—which resulted in excellent outcomes for investors. He then joined Great Hill Partners as the operating partner, working with seven portfolio companies on the boards of directors, as adviser to the CEOs, and, in one case, as interim CEO. He is now cofounder of a start-up called Madaket, an HCIT company based in Boston. He has served on the board of directors for twelve companies and five nonprofits. He is on the board of trustees for the Beth Israel Deaconess Medical Center, the Bright Spirit Children's Foundation, and the Foreign Policy Association.

Peter A. Garvin is the U.S. Navy military fellow at the Council on Foreign Relations in New York. He most recently commanded Patrol and Reconnaissance Wing Ten (CPRW-10) in Whidbey Island, Washington. He graduated with merit from the U.S. Naval Academy, earning a bachelor of science in aerospace engineering (astronautics track) in May 1989. He also holds a master of science in national security strategy from the National War College in Washington, DC. His operational assignments include Patrol Squadron Forty-five (VP-45), Patrol Squadron Five (VP-5), navigator aboard the amphibious assault ship USS *Kearsarge* (LHD-3), flag navigator for the embarked Amphibious Squadron Six, and executive and commanding officer of Patrol Squadron Eight (VP-8). During his operational tours he participated in Operations Noble Anvil, Shining Hope, Allied Force, Joint Guardian, Avid Response, Enduring Freedom, Iraqi Freedom, and New Dawn. Shore assignments include flag lieutenant to commander, Patrol Wings Atlantic, commander, Task Force Eighty-four (CTF-84); Patrol Squadron Thirty (VP-30); Washington, DC, placement officer at the Bureau of Naval Personnel; and executive assistant to the director, Operational Plans and Joint Force Development Directorate (J7) on the Joint Staff in Washington, DC.

Tressa Steffen Guenov is a professional staff member on the Senate Select Committee on Intelligence and is the committee designee for Senator Barbara Mikulski. She covers Syria, Israel, Palestine, Lebanon, Jordan, Egypt, and North Africa and supports the senator on cybersecurity issues. Previously, Guenov was the legislative assistant for national security affairs to Senator Claire McCaskill and supported her work on the Senate Armed Services Committee. Guenov worked on Central Asia issues in the Office of the Secretary of Defense, where she helped negotiate bilateral transit agreements to build the northern military supply lines into Afghanistan. She was a special assistant to the undersecretary of defense for policy (USDP) and the principal deputy USDP and served as a presidential management fellow at the State Department. Guenov also worked in several roles at the Center for Strategic and International Studies, including deputy director of the Commission on Science and Security. Guenov holds a BA, summa cum laude, from the University of Oregon and master's degrees from Oxford University and Washington University in St. Louis. She is a member of the Council on Foreign Relations, was a CFR term member, and served as co-chair of the Term Member Advisory Committee (2010–2012).

Emily McLeod is the deputy director for meetings in the Council on Foreign Relations' Washington Program. In this position, she manages a staff tasked with delivering intellectual content to CFR's Washington membership and the broader policy community, covering the most pressing international relations, national security, and international economic issues of the day. Over the course of her eight years at CFR, she has been involved in the planning and execution of more than one thousand CFR meetings, progressing to her current role of directing the overall substance, scope, and execution of a program aimed at the world's leading foreign policy practitioners and thinkers. She holds a BA in government with a concentration in leadership studies from Claremont McKenna College and a master's degree in international economics and strategic studies from Johns Hopkins University's School of Advanced International Studies (SAIS). While at SAIS, she served as the editor in chief of the *SAIS Review of International Affairs*. In 2012, she was named a Top 99 Under 33 Foreign Policy Leader by the *Diplomatic Courier* and Young Professionals in Foreign Policy.

Christopher A. Padilla has been vice president, governmental programs, at IBM Corporation since April 2009. Prior to joining IBM, Padilla served as undersecretary for international trade at the U.S. Department of Commerce, where he led the International Trade Administration. Before serving as undersecretary, Padilla was assistant secretary of commerce for export administration. From 2005 to 2006, he served as chief of staff and senior adviser to deputy secretary of state Robert B. Zoellick. From 2002 to 2005, he was assistant U.S. trade representative for intergovernmental affairs and public liaison, where he built support for trade agreements with nations in Latin America, Asia, and the Middle East. Padilla worked for more than fifteen years in the private sector prior to his government service. Over a ten-year career at AT&T and Lucent Technologies, he held a number of positions, including marketing, business development, and government affairs. Later, he was director of international trade relations at Eastman Kodak Company. He holds both a BA and an MA in international studies from Johns Hopkins University, where he was elected to Phi Beta Kappa. He serves on the boards of the Information Technology Industry Council, Council of the Americas, U.S.-India Business Council, and the YMCA of the USA.

Neal Reiter is a consultant with Booz Allen Hamilton in Silicon Valley. He uses technology to help solve problems related to big data, cybersecurity, and strategy formulation. He previously helped lead Booz Allen Hamilton's Cyber Intelligence Center, which is devoted to open-source intelligence and monitoring for the commercial marketplace. Previously, Reiter worked for Lockheed Martin, where he supported the military space division, including the Space-Based Infrared System (SBIRS), Advanced Extremely High Frequency (AEHF), and Transformational Satellite (TSAT) satellite constellations. Reiter received a BA in economics and philosophy from the University of California at Santa Barbara and a MBA from Yale University, where he was a Borg fellow.

Matthew C. Waxman is adjunct senior fellow for law and foreign policy at the Council on Foreign Relations. He is also a professor at Columbia Law School and a member of the Hoover Institution's task force on national security and law. He previously served at the U.S. Department of State as principal deputy director of policy planning. His prior government appointments include deputy assistant secretary of defense for detainee affairs, director for contingency planning and international justice at the National Security Council, and special assistant to the national security adviser. He is a graduate of Yale College and Yale Law School, and studied international relations as a Fulbright scholar in the United Kingdom. After law school, he served as law clerk to Supreme Court justice David H. Souter and U.S. Court of Appeals judge Joel M. Flaum. His publications include *The Dynamics of Coercion: American Foreign Policy and the Limits of Military Might* and the Council Special Report *Intervention to Stop Genocide and Mass Atrocities: International Norms and U.S. Policy.*

Independent Task Force Reports

Published by the Council on Foreign Relations

U.S.-Turkey Relations: A New Partnership
Madeleine K. Albright and Stephen J. Hadley, Chairs; Steven A. Cook, Project Director
Independent Task Force Report No. 69 (2012)

U.S. Education Reform and National Security
Joel I. Klein and Condoleezza Rice, Chairs; Julia Levy, Project Director
Independent Task Force Report No. 68 (2012)

U.S. Trade and Investment Policy
Andrew H. Card and Thomas A. Daschle, Chairs; Edward Alden and Matthew J. Slaughter,
Project Directors
Independent Task Force Report No. 67 (2011)

Global Brazil and U.S.-Brazil Relations
Samuel W. Bodman and James D. Wolfensohn, Chairs; Julia E. Sweig, Project Director
Independent Task Force Report No. 66 (2011)

U.S. Strategy for Pakistan and Afghanistan
Richard L. Armitage and Samuel R. Berger, Chairs; Daniel S. Markey, Project Director
Independent Task Force Report No. 65 (2010)

U.S. Policy Toward the Korean Peninsula
Charles L. Pritchard and John H. Tilelli Jr., Chairs; Scott A. Snyder, Project Director
Independent Task Force Report No. 64 (2010)

U.S. Immigration Policy
Jeb Bush and Thomas F. McLarty III, Chairs; Edward Alden, Project Director
Independent Task Force Report No. 63 (2009)

U.S. Nuclear Weapons Policy
William J. Perry and Brent Scowcroft, Chairs; Charles D. Ferguson, Project Director
Independent Task Force Report No. 62 (2009)

Confronting Climate Change: A Strategy for U.S. Foreign Policy
George E. Pataki and Thomas J. Vilsack, Chairs; Michael A. Levi, Project Director
Independent Task Force Report No. 61 (2008)

U.S.-Latin America Relations: A New Direction for a New Reality
Charlene Barshefsky and James T. Hill, Chairs; Shannon O'Neil, Project Director
Independent Task Force Report No. 60 (2008)

U.S.-China Relations: An Affirmative Agenda, A Responsible Course
Carla A. Hills and Dennis C. Blair, Chairs; Frank Sampson Jannuzi, Project Director
Independent Task Force Report No. 59 (2007)

National Security Consequences of U.S. Oil Dependency
John Deutch and James R. Schlesinger, Chairs; David G. Victor, Project Director
Independent Task Force Report No. 58 (2006)

Russia's Wrong Direction: What the United States Can and Should Do
John Edwards and Jack Kemp, Chairs; Stephen Sestanovich, Project Director
Independent Task Force Report No. 57 (2006)

More than Humanitarianism: A Strategic U.S. Approach Toward Africa
Anthony Lake and Christine Todd Whitman, Chairs; Princeton N. Lyman and J. Stephen
Morrison, Project Directors
Independent Task Force Report No. 56 (2006)

In the Wake of War: Improving Post-Conflict Capabilities
Samuel R. Berger and Brent Scowcroft, Chairs; William L. Nash, Project Director; Mona K.
Sutphen, Deputy Director
Independent Task Force Report No. 55 (2005)

In Support of Arab Democracy: Why and How
Madeleine K. Albright and Vin Weber, Chairs; Steven A. Cook, Project Director
Independent Task Force Report No. 54 (2005)

Building a North American Community
John P. Manley, Pedro Aspe, and William F. Weld, Chairs; Thomas d'Aquino, Andrés
Rozental, and Robert Pastor, Vice Chairs; Chappell H. Lawson, Project Director
Independent Task Force Report No. 53 (2005)

Iran: Time for a New Approach
Zbigniew Brzezinski and Robert M. Gates, Chairs; Suzanne Maloney, Project Director
Independent Task Force Report No. 52 (2004)

An Update on the Global Campaign Against Terrorist Financing
Maurice R. Greenberg, Chair; William F. Wechsler and Lee S. Wolosky, Project Directors
Independent Task Force Report No. 40B (Web-only release, 2004)

Renewing the Atlantic Partnership
Henry A. Kissinger and Lawrence H. Summers, Chairs; Charles A. Kupchan, Project Director
Independent Task Force Report No. 51 (2004)

Iraq: One Year After
Thomas R. Pickering and James R. Schlesinger, Chairs; Eric P. Schwartz, Project Consultant
Independent Task Force Report No. 43C (Web-only release, 2004)

Nonlethal Weapons and Capabilities
Paul X. Kelley and Graham Allison, Chairs; Richard L. Garwin, Project Director
Independent Task Force Report No. 50 (2004)

New Priorities in South Asia: U.S. Policy Toward India, Pakistan, and Afghanistan
(Chairmen's Report)
Marshall Bouton, Nicholas Platt, and Frank G. Wisner, Chairs; Dennis Kux and Mahnaz
Ispahani, Project Directors
Independent Task Force Report No. 49 (2003)
Cosponsored with the Asia Society

Finding America's Voice: A Strategy for Reinvigorating U.S. Public Diplomacy
Peter G. Peterson, Chair; Kathy Bloomgarden, Henry Grunwald, David E. Morey, and
Shibley Telhami, Working Committee Chairs; Jennifer Sieg, Project Director; Sharon
Herbstman, Project Coordinator
Independent Task Force Report No. 48 (2003)

Emergency Responders: Drastically Underfunded, Dangerously Unprepared
Warren B. Rudman, Chair; Richard A. Clarke, Senior Adviser; Jamie F. Metzl,
Project Director
Independent Task Force Report No. 47 (2003)

Iraq: The Day After (Chairs' Update)
Thomas R. Pickering and James R. Schlesinger, Chairs; Eric P. Schwartz, Project Director
Independent Task Force Report No. 43B (Web-only release, 2003)

Burma: Time for Change
Mathea Falco, Chair
Independent Task Force Report No. 46 (2003)

Afghanistan: Are We Losing the Peace?
Marshall Bouton, Nicholas Platt, and Frank G. Wisner, Chairs; Dennis Kux and Mahnaz
Ispahani, Project Directors
Chairman's Report of an Independent Task Force (2003)
Cosponsored with the Asia Society

Meeting the North Korean Nuclear Challenge
Morton I. Abramowitz and James T. Laney, Chairs; Eric Heginbotham, Project Director
Independent Task Force Report No. 45 (2003)

Chinese Military Power
Harold Brown, Chair; Joseph W. Prueher, Vice Chair; Adam Segal, Project Director
Independent Task Force Report No. 44 (2003)

Iraq: The Day After
Thomas R. Pickering and James R. Schlesinger, Chairs; Eric P. Schwartz, Project Director
Independent Task Force Report No. 43 (2003)

Threats to Democracy: Prevention and Response
Madeleine K. Albright and Bronislaw Geremek, Chairs; Morton H. Halperin, Director;
Elizabeth Frawley Bagley, Associate Director
Independent Task Force Report No. 42 (2002)

America—Still Unprepared, Still in Danger
Gary Hart and Warren B. Rudman, Chairs; Stephen E. Flynn, Project Director
Independent Task Force Report No. 41 (2002)

Terrorist Financing
Maurice R. Greenberg, Chair; William F. Wechsler and Lee S. Wolosky, Project Directors
Independent Task Force Report No. 40 (2002)

Enhancing U.S. Leadership at the United Nations
David Dreier and Lee H. Hamilton, Chairs; Lee Feinstein and Adrian Karatnycky, Project
Directors
Independent Task Force Report No. 39 (2002)
Cosponsored with Freedom House

Improving the U.S. Public Diplomacy Campaign in the War Against Terrorism
Carla A. Hills and Richard C. Holbrooke, Chairs; Charles G. Boyd, Project Director
Independent Task Force Report No. 38 (Web-only release, 2001)

Building Support for More Open Trade
Kenneth M. Duberstein and Robert E. Rubin, Chairs; Timothy F. Geithner, Project Director;
Daniel R. Lucich, Deputy Project Director
Independent Task Force Report No. 37 (2001)

Beginning the Journey: China, the United States, and the WTO
Robert D. Hormats, Chair; Elizabeth Economy and Kevin Nealer, Project Directors
Independent Task Force Report No. 36 (2001)

Strategic Energy Policy Update
Edward L. Morse, Chair; Amy Myers Jaffe, Project Director
Independent Task Force Report No. 33B (2001)
Cosponsored with the James A. Baker III Institute for Public Policy of Rice University

Testing North Korea: The Next Stage in U.S. and ROK Policy
Morton I. Abramowitz and James T. Laney, Chairs; Robert A. Manning, Project Director
Independent Task Force Report No. 35 (2001)

The United States and Southeast Asia: A Policy Agenda for the New Administration
J. Robert Kerrey, Chair; Robert A. Manning, Project Director
Independent Task Force Report No. 34 (2001)

Strategic Energy Policy: Challenges for the 21st Century
Edward L. Morse, Chair; Amy Myers Jaffe, Project Director
Independent Task Force Report No. 33 (2001)
Cosponsored with the James A. Baker III Institute for Public Policy of Rice University

A Letter to the President and a Memorandum on U.S. Policy Toward Brazil
Stephen Robert, Chair; Kenneth Maxwell, Project Director
Independent Task Force Report No. 32 (2001)

State Department Reform
Frank C. Carlucci, Chair; Ian J. Brzezinski, Project Coordinator
Independent Task Force Report No. 31 (2001)
Cosponsored with the Center for Strategic and International Studies

U.S.-Cuban Relations in the 21st Century: A Follow-on Report
Bernard W. Aronson and William D. Rogers, Chairs; Julia Sweig and Walter Mead, Project Directors
Independent Task Force Report No. 30 (2000)

Toward Greater Peace and Security in Colombia: Forging a Constructive U.S. Policy
Bob Graham and Brent Scowcroft, Chairs; Michael Shifter, Project Director
Independent Task Force Report No. 29 (2000)
Cosponsored with the Inter-American Dialogue

Future Directions for U.S. Economic Policy Toward Japan
Laura D'Andrea Tyson, Chair; M. Diana Helweg Newton, Project Director
Independent Task Force Report No. 28 (2000)

First Steps Toward a Constructive U.S. Policy in Colombia
Bob Graham and Brent Scowcroft, Chairs; Michael Shifter, Project Director
Interim Report (2000)
Cosponsored with the Inter-American Dialogue

Promoting Sustainable Economies in the Balkans
Steven Rattner, Chair; Michael B.G. Froman, Project Director
Independent Task Force Report No. 27 (2000)

Non-Lethal Technologies: Progress and Prospects
Richard L. Garwin, Chair; W. Montague Winfield, Project Director
Independent Task Force Report No. 26 (1999)

Safeguarding Prosperity in a Global Financial System:
The Future International Financial Architecture
Carla A. Hills and Peter G. Peterson, Chairs; Morris Goldstein, Project Director
Independent Task Force Report No. 25 (1999)
Cosponsored with the International Institute for Economics

U.S. Policy Toward North Korea: Next Steps
Morton I. Abramowitz and James T. Laney, Chairs; Michael J. Green, Project Director
Independent Task Force Report No. 24 (1999)

Reconstructing the Balkans
Morton I. Abramowitz and Albert Fishlow, Chairs; Charles A. Kupchan, Project Director
Independent Task Force Report No. 23 (Web-only release, 1999)

Strengthening Palestinian Public Institutions
Michel Rocard, Chair; Henry Siegman, Project Director; Yezid Sayigh and Khalil Shikaki, Principal Authors
Independent Task Force Report No. 22 (1999)

U.S. Policy Toward Northeastern Europe
Zbigniew Brzezinski, Chair; F. Stephen Larrabee, Project Director
Independent Task Force Report No. 21 (1999)

The Future of Transatlantic Relations
Robert D. Blackwill, Chair and Project Director
Independent Task Force Report No. 20 (1999)

U.S.-Cuban Relations in the 21st Century
Bernard W. Aronson and William D. Rogers, Chairs; Walter Russell Mead, Project Director
Independent Task Force Report No. 19 (1999)

After the Tests: U.S. Policy Toward India and Pakistan
Richard N. Haass and Morton H. Halperin, Chairs
Independent Task Force Report No. 18 (1998)
Cosponsored with the Brookings Institution

Managing Change on the Korean Peninsula
Morton I. Abramowitz and James T. Laney, Chairs; Michael J. Green, Project Director
Independent Task Force Report No. 17 (1998)

Promoting U.S. Economic Relations with Africa
Peggy Dulany and Frank Savage, Chairs; Salih Booker, Project Director
Independent Task Force Report No. 16 (1998)

U.S. Middle East Policy and the Peace Process
Henry Siegman, Project Coordinator
Independent Task Force Report No. 15 (1997)

Differentiated Containment: U.S. Policy Toward Iran and Iraq
Zbigniew Brzezinski and Brent Scowcroft, Chairs; Richard W. Murphy, Project Director
Independent Task Force Report No. 14 (1997)

Russia, Its Neighbors, and an Enlarging NATO
Richard G. Lugar, Chair; Victoria Nuland, Project Director
Independent Task Force Report No. 13 (1997)

Rethinking International Drug Control: New Directions for U.S. Policy
Mathea Falco, Chair
Independent Task Force Report No. 12 (1997)

Financing America's Leadership: Protecting American Interests and Promoting American Values
Mickey Edwards and Stephen J. Solarz, Chairs; Morton H. Halperin, Lawrence J. Korb,
and Richard M. Moose, Project Directors
Independent Task Force Report No. 11 (1997)
Cosponsored with the Brookings Institution

A New U.S. Policy Toward India and Pakistan
Richard N. Haass, Chair; Gideon Rose, Project Director
Independent Task Force Report No. 10 (1997)

Arms Control and the U.S.-Russian Relationship
Robert D. Blackwill, Chair and Author; Keith W. Dayton, Project Director
Independent Task Force Report No. 9 (1996)
Cosponsored with the Nixon Center for Peace and Freedom

American National Interest and the United Nations
George Soros, Chair
Independent Task Force Report No. 8 (1996)

Making Intelligence Smarter: The Future of U.S. Intelligence
Maurice R. Greenberg, Chair; Richard N. Haass, Project Director
Independent Task Force Report No. 7 (1996)

Lessons of the Mexican Peso Crisis
John C. Whitehead, Chair; Marie-Josée Kravis, Project Director
Independent Task Force Report No. 6 (1996)

Managing the Taiwan Issue: Key Is Better U.S. Relations with China
Stephen Friedman, Chair; Elizabeth Economy, Project Director
Independent Task Force Report No. 5 (1995)

Non-Lethal Technologies: Military Options and Implications
Malcolm H. Wiener, Chair
Independent Task Force Report No. 4 (1995)

Should NATO Expand?
Harold Brown, Chair; Charles A. Kupchan, Project Director
Independent Task Force Report No. 3 (1995)

Success or Sellout? The U.S.-North Korean Nuclear Accord
Kyung Won Kim and Nicholas Platt, Chairs; Richard N. Haass, Project Director
Independent Task Force Report No. 2 (1995)
Cosponsored with the Seoul Forum for International Affairs

Nuclear Proliferation: Confronting the New Challenges
Stephen J. Hadley, Chair; Mitchell B. Reiss, Project Director
Independent Task Force Report No. 1 (1995)

Note: Task Force reports are available for download from CFR's website, www.cfr.org.
For more information, email publications@cfr.org.